THE
POWER
OF
Resurrection
LIVING

BE ATTUNED TO GOD'S LOVING PRESENCE
AND TRANSFORMING POWER

ETHAN JAMES

LifeRich Publishing is a registered trademark of The Reader's Digest Association, Inc.

LifeRich Publishing books may be ordered through booksellers or by contacting:

LifeRich Publishing
1663 Liberty Drive
Bloomington, IN 47403
www.liferichpublishing.com
844-686-9607

ISBN: 978-1-4897-5005-1 (sc)
ISBN: 978-1-4897-5007-5 (hc)
ISBN: 978-1-4897-5006-8 (e)

Library of Congress Control Number: 2024900391

Print information available on the last page.

LifeRich Publishing rev. date: 01/30/2024

To those in whom the resurrected Christ has revealed Himself to me: my wife Sue, and our amazing, loving, and supportive family; the churches I've had the wonderful privilege of pastoring—Amber Street Baptist Church, Flower Bluff, Texas; First Southern Baptist Church, Oakland, California; Calvary Baptist Church, Hayward, California; and Turlock Community Fellowship, Turlock, California; the Band of Brothers in Modesto and Turlock; and the most courageous people I have been blessed to know, my clients.

What you do with your attention is in the
end what you do with your life.
—John Green

Contents

Preface xiii

Acknowledgments xv

Introduction xvii

Chapter 1   Expedition: A Journey into Authentic Living 1

Chapter 2   Resurrection Living and Grief:
             Learning to Live Without 19

Chapter 3   Wisdom, Good Sense, and Sound Judgment 28

Chapter 4   Attending: Being Present with or
             Aware of Another 48

Chapter 5   Musings: A Time of Reflection or Thought 59

Chapter 6   Resurrection: The State of One
             Awakened from Death 121

Appendix A: Negative Perception List 151

Appendix B: "All the Names of Jesus" Link 153

Appendix C: How to Create a Gratitude Journal 155

Appendix D: Enhancing Personal Worship 157

Appendix E: Small Group Leader's Guide 159

Appendix F: Stages of Loss 161
Appendix G: Care-Taking Instead of Caregiving 165
Endnotes 167
Bibliography 173
About the Author.. 177

Preface

Bart said of the song, "I Can Only Imagine," "The lyrics took about ten minutes."

Amy Grant replied, "You didn't write this song in ten minutes. It took a lifetime."

The work you have in your hands took a lifetime of failures, dead-end dreams, a fractured family, God-encounters, and remarkable life-experiences. The journey of writing began years ago out of how much God has given me: the insights, wisdom, and knowledge gained through clients, groups, churches, and family. They are life-changing for me. I felt an obligation to God and those in my life to put on the page these thoughts to share with you.

Acknowledgments

Alone, we can do so little; together, we can do so much.

—Helen Keller

My heartfelt appreciation to my wife, Sue, and our family for their patience, love, and support. To my brother, Randy, who graciously provided motels and transportation in my hometown, Houston, so I could spend private time to work on the book. To my nephew Curtis, inviting me to spend time on his scenic and tranquil Caribbean beachfront property on Ambergris Caye so I could reflect and write. To Debbie, for spelling and grammar. To the Band of Brothers in Turlock and in Modesto for their encouragement, insights, and wisdom. To the churches I've pastored, especially Turlock Community Fellowship, the most authentic, continuous community which has impacted my life and the world. To the clients, who were heroic in facing and conquering the sufferings they experienced. To the intercessors who loved me through prayer in this project. And most profoundly, to Jesus Christ, the Gift He is and those companions He has given on this journey.

Introduction

I am the resurrection and the life.

—Jesus

Joni Eareckson Tada, author, singer, artist, radio personality, and advocate for the disabled, when asked in an interview by Dr. Tim Clinton, how she coped with being a quadriplegic, said, "I have come to know *His* presence is enough."[1]

In the challenges of life, we can live in God's presence to discover He is setting each of us free to be the person He created for an authentic, Christlike life.

The mind is the brain at work, and we can exercise our brain like any other muscle in our body. We can use challenging crossword puzzles, brain games, or math questions. We can also train our brain to be more attentive to God

This is a story of a deeply broken man who is discovering God's presence is the most precious thing in the world and, because of God's presence, lives are impacted beyond what he could imagine.

Chapter 1 is a personal story of learning to experience the abundant life in Christ and the creation of a tiny community that impacted the world.

Chapter 2 shows God meeting me in the depth of significant loss.

Chapter 3 explains how we can change our thinking, which transforms our faith and our relationship to God and others.

Chapter 4 explores the positive influence gratitude and praise can have on us and shares scriptures we can use to reframe our thinking.

Chapter 5 provides scriptures and questions that will help us become more aware of God's presence in our daily life.

Chapter 6 chronicles a journey. Following Christ into resurrection living can be personally costly and yet have significant influence in our world.

Explanations of brain basics and scripture reflections, along with insights and questions, will enable you to be more intentional in God's company in your daily life.

Resources are provided in the appendixes for further help in your journey.

One

EXPEDITION: A JOURNEY INTO AUTHENTIC LIVING

> Authenticity: The courage to be yourself.
> —Anonymous

I am a poster child for complex posttraumatic disorder. Imagine you are a five-year-old kid in the middle of war. You're scantily clothed and malnourished, attempting to keep yourself and a woman alive. Trying to hide, you and she are relentlessly pursued, discovered, and wounded. One misstep could wipe you out; land mines and booby traps have been concealed throughout the landscape. The wounds go so deep you think they will never heal. All this is executed by an enemy who has betrayed you both. The reason for the battle: you. You are the cause of the conflict, suffering, and unhappiness.

Now you're a teenager, feeling abandoned and trying to make your way through the minefield of daily living. Profound shame haunts your every move. You cannot need; you are unworthy. You can't grasp the rules of healthy relationships. Still clutching your shredded clothing, you try to make the best of it. You fake it, always smile, and placate so "they" won't know what you are: toxic.

Now, as an adult, you only have faint mental images of all these things. However, you swing between feeling numb and experiencing mental flooding or between feeling numb and experiencing emotional distress storms, and you don't know why.

However, I am discovering God has the power to transform trauma into the wonder of intimacy and the seedbed of blessings for others, even when the wounds are caused by an unpredictable, violent alcoholic father and an overly dependent mother.

Resurrection living is an ongoing activity in which the Holy Spirit reclaims our wounds, failures, sorrows, missteps, and abandonments, transforming them into a source of God's intended creative purpose in us: being Christlike.

The Winchester Mystery House in San Jose, California, contains more than one hundred rooms of confusing construction. Stairs wind up to the celling, door after door opens to nothing or to more doors, and windows open to walls or other windows. Chaos indeed.

I could not have known as a ten-year-old that I was signing the title deed of my life over to His Lordship. It gradually dawned on me He expected to occupy every area for which Christ had paid such a high price: the household of me and my life. No matter how long it was going to take or how much I would protest, He was going to rearrange every room and hidden, closed, and dark corner I declared as my own. What the Holy Spirit wanted from me in this renovation was a teachable heart. And *that* spirit was not going to be easy for me to surrender.

A taped message by Millard Baux was an epiphany for me. The insight became the lodestar of the Holy Spirit's movement in my life and the lives of so many. Millard stood before six hundred people during a Wednesday night prayer meeting at his church in Houston, Texas, and proclaimed, "I would rather be on the top of a sand dune in the middle of God's will than pastor the largest church in Texas." Through a series of hilarious, God-ordered events, 160 days later he was pastoring a church in Yuma, Arizona. After some time griping and grumbling before the Lord, Millard shared the following conversation with Him.

"Millard, do you know why you're here?"

"No, Lord, I have no idea."

"I want you to drive out to the middle of the desert."

According to Millard, he drove around the desert for some time, wondering why he was out there. He finally found two palm trees in the shape of a large V in the middle of nowhere. He sat under them because he did not know what else to do.

The Lord said, "Millard, can you explain how these palm trees exist in the middle of nowhere?"

Millard replied, "No, Lord, I can't."

"Go home and find out about palm trees."

Millard discovered palm trees have a deep taproot burrowing to a water source.

The Lord said, "Now, Millard, do you understand why you're here?"

"No, Lord."

"Just like those palm trees that have deep roots into an unknown water source, I desire to be your water source. You are here to discover I am your life in inexplicable ways. I want to be inside you and before others as your fount of spirituality and life."[1]

Here's the beginning of God's reclamation process as He became the fount of spirituality and life.

In 1957, I was seventeen, sitting on a grassy knoll at Trinity Lakes Baptist Camp outside Austin, Texas. I listened to a challenge to yield to the Lord's ministry. Call it a vision, a dream, or exhaustion: I saw hundreds of people looking at me, their eyes filled with the pain of deprivation. I interpreted the vision as doing something great for

3

the Lord, like becoming another Billy Graham! God displayed His patient loving-kindness as He destroyed the tightly grasped illusion. I was driven to see that my egocentric definition of greatness and God's were radically at odds. Much later I realized these people hungered to know a deeper, more meaningful, intimate relationship with God. To live more consistently in His presence.

The next year, inside an immense tent and perspiring in the heat of a Mississippi summer, I was gripped by the messages on the deeper life of Christ. "I am crucified with Christ: nevertheless I live; yet not I, but Christ liveth in me" (Galatians 2:20 KJV). Christ saved us to live His life in and through us. Fifteen hundred Southern Baptists had gathered at Mount Zion Baptist Camp in Myrtle, Mississippi. They were raising their hands and swaying to the praise music. Some stood before the raised platform at the front, weeping.

My educated senses insulted, I stalked out and ascended a small hill. There, God assaulted my conscience: "Whose life are you going to live, yours or Mine?"

I broke emotionally. Sobbing, I fell on my knees, repelled by my self-centeredness. The truth ran over me like a freight train. I had a choice: to live my life on my terms or to renounce my arrogance and embrace Jesus's life in and through me. Running back into the tent and down the aisle, I planted myself in the arms of Pastor Percy Ray, the director of the camp. I blubbered out my capitulation; I wanted to know His life in me. He responded, "Son, this is just the beginning."

I could not have known how deeply the Holy Spirit would plow into those wounds, nor how long it would take to uncover and free me from the lies I believed about myself. He gently yet persistently compelled me to bare these hurts to individuals, groups, and congregations with which I was involved. In the arduous journey of authenticity, these injuries become sources of life and healing to me and others. "When our wounds cease to be a source of shame and become a source of healing, we have become wounded healers," expounds Henri Nouwen.[2]

God was subpoenaing me to die to the control driven by the lies I desperately clung to and to be drawn to intimacy with Him.

In 1960, attending Corpus Christi Baptist University, I met and fell in love with Sue, this extraordinary woman who became my wife and whose lifelong companionship and encouragement helped make this amazing adventure possible. Sorrowfully, after years of living with agonizing rheumatoid arthritis and being diagnosed with midstage Alzheimer's in April 2020, my precious wife of fifty-nine years died in our home on January 2, 2021.

It was a miraculous end and coronation of a woman whose life has had a lasting effect on our extended family. For more than forty years she was an inspiration to parents and children as a teacher and preschool director.

Through this sorrow, God's Spirit has given me the precious gift of examination. The word has its roots in Latin, referring to the scale on a balance: the idea came to mean the precise review of the truth in the situation. It is in this gift I have come to know God's heart and mine. I am compelled to offer this gift to you as you read through this work.

In 1962, I was asked to pastor of the Amber Street Baptist Church in Flour Bluff, Texas, a dying congregation with the intention of closing the building and reopening as a Spanish mission. Five disheartened people met with me the first Sunday. Filled with pain created by a former pastor, they felt hopeless and visionless.

My memory fails as to how things changed, but they did. People returned, and new people came and were saved. Church attendance grew, missions were supported, and the building was refurbished. The Spanish congregation met there on Sunday afternoons. The church sponsored a radio program reaching the greater Corpus

Christi area. God began to echo the message to my soul. "This is My life in you and in the church I desire."

In 1964, I attended seminary in Mill Valley, California. At the same time, I was invited to lead another fellowship of lost dreams and hopes: First Southern Baptist Church, Oakland. Sixteen dear people were fighting to stay alive in the downtown area. Burdened by the church, I drove into the hills above the city and parked, overlooking a community of over seventy-five thousand lost people.

"Lord, how can we reach so many? There's so much need here."

I was reminded of what Jesus said to His followers before sending them to great need (Matthew 9:35–10:1). He whispered, "I did not call you to needs. I called you to Myself. I will move through you to meet the needs by who I am, not by who you think you are."

A renewed life returned. Mission became the driving force in the membership. An active outreach was created, baptizing more lost souls than ever before in the history of the church. Bible study grew along with attendance. With a palpable sense of joy and expectation, members began to believe their church could make a difference in downtown Oakland.

In 1969, I was twenty-nine and much more aware of God's life in me. I became pastor of Calvary Baptist Church in Hayward, a church with depleted attendance, hope, and life. Once again, God's life broke through the despair. Within six months, the church began to turn around.

Then the Department of Motor Vehicles restricted my driving to daytime because of vision problems. I saw this as death to my "successful" ministry. As an overachiever driven by insecurity, I was terrified of letting these people down.

Since Sue was busy taking care of our children, I had to ask people in the congregation to drive me to visits, witnessing, ministering, and speaking.

As I shared my heart and vision with them, trust and love flourished. As they watched me, they began to emulate what I was doing. The members realized they were called on mission to minister in the marketplace, neighborhood, and world. The church had various groups working in and serving the community at large – Bible studies, women's care and share groups, training clusters for issues of addiction and other personal problems, financial budgeting training teams for families and individuals.

Mission giving was increased to 33 percent of the church budget.

I felt there was no need to preach on tithing. Members involved in ministry realize they are on mission with God in their daily life and financial commitment.

Mission is an inevitable expression of resurrection living. God is on mission, in our homes, churches, neighborhoods, marketplaces and world. Christ, living His life through us, summons us to join with Him and His Father in His work, wherever that may be. "I do the works of my Father" (John 10:37).

Here it's important we understand mission.

Mission: an assigned trust borne for the glory of God. The moment we are saved, we are entrusted by God to be enabled by the Holy Spirit to live out the life of Christ, nothing less.

Individuals gifted in listening and compassion ministered to the broken and the lost. A deacon who'd grown up in back of a mortuary realized God could use his experience as a gift. After training he became the Deacon to the Dying. Families with developmentally disabled children started attending, providing a ministry opportunity to the parents and their children. More people were baptized as a result of these ministries than from my efforts.

In 1976, a church in Turlock, California, invited me to be their pastor. They were impressed with the growth at Calvary and wanted me to help them increase their membership. God made it clear, I was to go.

What I didn't understand was those in power wanted me to help them grow by adding people who would sustain their image in the community, people just like them. Within months, individuals from different socioeconomic backgrounds began attending the church.

The old guard criticized my preaching, creating conflicts over programs and budget. I lost all sense of confidence. But I stayed for six and a half years. When the situation became untenable, I offered my resignation.

In September 1982, the Turlock Community Fellowship was birthed with fifty people who desired more than what the traditional church offered. They were captured by the vision of being involved in the activity of God in their everyday lives.

After prayer and counsel with the state leadership, I agreed to be their pastor. Within ten days we gained sponsorship as a mission and found a place to meet and worship: a roller rink.

I established Sonburst Counseling Service offering help for individuals and couples, which made it possible for the church to use its funds for mission and ministry. Because the members carried the church's ministries, I was able to offer my assistance to the Turlock Police Department as chaplain and write a weekly advice column in a local newspaper, the *Manteca Bulletin*.

These trained and enabled members developed ministries such as Women of Early Sexual Trauma meetings, relational Bible studies, a Sunday night call-in talk program staffed by members, a couple fostering dying children, a Christ-centered Big Brother/Big Sister program, and a weekly food donation skate program supporting three community food banks.

A major feature of the church's ministry was working with developmentally disabled adults and providing ministry opportunity for them. These "special people" were an incredible gift to our fellowship.

The church established a monthly Bible study meeting of the developmentally disabled from throughout the county. Birthed from this group was the Joy Sounds Choir for "special folk" to sing in churches and the malls throughout the Central Valley and before the state legislature.

The following is a letter written to our local newspaper, the *Turlock Journal*, on July 27, 1987:

> Dear Editor,
>
> I am the mother of a young man who is mentally retarded and through the years I have experienced many personal moments of hurt concerning reactions from the "normal public." I believe that special recognition should be given to individuals and organizations who accept people that are different because they care.
>
> I myself do not attend church and have some very opinionated feelings concerning the benefits of organized religion. I do, however, feel that out of all the churches in Turlock, one in particular deserves some recognition because it accepts with open arms and equal membership all afflictions. Each Sunday, I take my son and leave him for Bible Study and church services. He looks forward to this as do many others like him who attend and are accepted as equals with the rest of the congregation.

I am referring to the Turlock Community Fellowship. My understanding is that the fellowship is part of the Orangeburg Baptist Church of Modesto, and was established in the latter part of 1982, as an alternative to traditional churches. TCF has no fancy building and services are held at the Rec Center, a roller rink here in Turlock. There are no statues to remind people that God is present nor do they repeatedly pass a collection plate or ask families to donate time and money for their existence.

In addition to church services, TCF, together with the Christian Berets, and other groups and churches, supports the Joy Sounds Choir. This choir is directed by Valerie and Howard Lower of Turlock, and is composed of a group of 35 to 45 "special" young people, both physically, and/or mentally handicapped. They have been singing for years for area churches and groups, the California Legislature and during the Christmas Season, at a mall in Modesto.

I realize that the Turlock Community Fellowship also has many other phases of interest but one concern rests with their interest in our children who have been rejected by others in life.

I believe that the *Turlock Journal* that covers so many other religious events should consider sending a reporter to visit and do a public interest story on this group which practices what others just preach.[2]

A year later, editor Poly McNabb of The California Southern

Baptist, our state paper, spent Sunday in worship and interviewed the members. In the article she described many of the ministries. In her editorial, Polly referred to a book by J. Terry Young, *The Church Alive and Growing.*

She noted his comment regarding hospitals having special care units, "Wouldn't be wonderful if God's people, the church, could look after each other in such a fashion."

She further cited, "We must stand humbly before the Scriptures, expecting God to speak to us in yet sharper and deeper insight instead of arrogantly assuming we already have all the answers and there is nothing new to learn."

She then said, "The church is not a sanctimonious society for the self-righteous. It is a hospital for sick souls where the Holy Spirit employs a type of group therapy using spiritually sick people to help each other to higher levels of Christian growth and maturity."

Polly concluded, "As I sat in the congregation of Turlock Community Fellowship on a recent Sunday, I immediately thought of what Dr. Young had written. I realized I was seeing a church in action such as he described in his book. And a happier group of people I have yet to meet."[3]

In 1989 several major families left us. The reason: we would not be investing funds for a church building. We planned to stay in the roller rink to be more effective in reaching the unchurched and using our funds for missions.

In 1990, we were invited to meet in a facility for developmentally disabled adults by the same lady who wrote to the *Turlock Journal.* As we continued to be a church without walls, we realize pretension can't last in such an environment which creates a humble and mutual accountability among ourselves. It's hard to explain or define, but community takes on a life of its own and creates its own path in relation to Christ and to each other.

We continued to struggle with others leaving, finances, and lack of attendance. On several occasions we even considered closing. "Body Talks" were an opportunity for everyone to be open concerning their thoughts and feelings in a "no holds barred" session. In the midst of all pain, anger, frustration, and indifference, the membership went on its knees in desperate intercession.

As the fellowship prayed, we made the difficult decision of closing down many of our ministries and give ourselves to extended times of prayer.

The openness along with prayer became our very lifeblood, creating a cohesive existence we came to know as authentic community.

"If we are going to use the word (community) meaningfully we must restrict to a group of individuals who have learned how to communicate honestly with each other, whose relationships go deeper than their mask of composure, and who have developed some significant commitment to 'rejoice together, mourn together,' and to 'delight in each other, make others' condition our own,'" offers M. Scott Peck.[4]

The issue I constantly faced as pastor was to be sensitive to the Spirit's path and create an open and safe environment for the community to respond as the Spirit led, no matter how difficult or uncomfortable.

Driving to work, I complained that not only had we lost all those families, we were not seeing growth in attendance. I was reminded that when Moses struck the rock out of anger instead of speaking to it, he robbed the glory from God. It was that character flaw, taking God's place, which prevented him from entering the Promised Land. If there, he would be tempted to do the same thing.

God was keeping TCF tiny for His glory to display how big *He* was. Moreover, He knew my propensity to want to do things my way, getting me the attention.

I was so overwhelmed with gratitude, I pulled the car over and began to weep.

As we focused on prayer seeking God's direction, we studied the first three chapters of Revelation on Sunday evenings. Using Walter Wink's *Transforming Bible Study: A Leader's Guide*, we accepted the angel of the church was real. For six weeks, through interactive activities, study, and prayer, the group formulated the following letter which was then shared with the body.

Letter to the Angel of Turlock
Community Fellowship

I have found you faithful and I am pleased with you. Lay down your brokenness before Me as your gift to Me. The wounded-ness of the past and the future wounded-ness have purpose. The reason for your pain is to draw you to My heart. Be confident, I am in control, this is the source of your joy. Others have called you "losers" or "misfits" but in this you will come to recognize your hidden strength.

Continue to build community through the accountability and brokenness that is among you. Focus on Me as your First Love. As you do so, those who desperately seek Me will be drawn to you. Come to recognize each person I bring to you as a unique gift.

Intercessory prayer is the essence of My call, continue and I will send you to higher places. It is in this work you represent Me. It is in this mystery of intercession I create My meeting place to encounter you and rest Myself upon you. Surrender the dark places you experience as precious to Me. Therefore, you are not to be ashamed, fearful or timid.

Above all, your worship of Me defines who you are as a church and it is out of this worship which comes your confidence and joy.

Out of this time of self-examination and prayer, it became clear we were being called to something God-sized.

With the loss of so many families leaving and thirty-five people in attendance, we began to sustain the larger body of Christ though on-site intercession, consulting on the work of reconciliation and financial support. In eleven years TCF was enabled to commit over $900,000 to mission work in California; other states; Northern Ireland; South Korea; Coventry England; South Africa; India; Cambodia; and Israel/Palestine reconciliation activities. We have through benevolence supported single women, mentoring pastors, and businesspeople and financed a Christian artist/poet who has impacted her world for Christ.

A major part of the financial support came from Sonburst clients. I never talked them about these ministry opportunities or asked for money. God had convinced us as a fellowship to pray concerning these challenges, and He would supply the resources, which He always did.

I feel it's important for you to grasp the immensity of God's activity in a tiny community of believers. Two situations convey clearly the extent of His activity.

Julie, a widow in our church and Spanish teacher in one of the toughest schools in a city in the central valley, was burdened for missions. She held a weekly Bible study, which at times overflowed the classroom. Yet she yearned for more.

Searching the internet, she found a ministry in Pakistan and Kerala, India, the Zion Gospel Church, a mid-caste Pentecostal work which has established seventeen churches in this southern state. Emails back and forth convinced her she needed to go. The challenge: a full-time teacher, finances, and critical family members who said she was not qualified to go.

She shared her burden with the church, and after a week of intensive prayer, we decided to send her. The funds had been supplied, and she traveled to these countries during Christmas break.

She returned satisfied we were to support this creditable Pentecostal organization in Kerala. A team went to Kerala four times to help train the pastors, lead their annual conference, and encourage the local churches.

The following is an email we received in June 2018 from Joseph Binoy, director of the seventeen churches in the area. "My mind recaps all blessed times when I write this mail. I had friendship with Sis Julie in 2005. Thus I came to know about you and TCF through her."

He listed the results of the church's financial support: purchased cemetery in seven places for Christian burial, four pieces of land for new church halls, construction of six church halls, sleeping quarters for orphans (during the daytime they are used as school rooms for training pastors), funds for fifteen motorcycles, a vehicle, and food for the needy and victims of monsoon season.

The second is a mission in Cambodia led by two people, twenty years ago were told they too old to go. We became aware of them through a couple in TCF.

Dearest Pastor,

God called us to go to Cambodia in January, 2002. Little did we know what all God was going to do, and who He was going to draw into this circle of making it possible to show His Mercy and Love to the amazing people of Cambodia.

Not only the Grace of God, but also through a body of believers who were open to listen to the Holy Spirit as God would bless TCF with most unusual finances to be used to funnel at the Holy Spirit's direction.

First it came for monthly support for six of our pastors starting in 2005 and lasting for 12 years. This helped them to be able to go out and establish Churches and raise up leadership. The fruit still goes on.

We were able to purchase 55 motorbikes through the $50,000 that came from TCF. This empowered our leaders to be able to go out into the Harvest Field as they were led. These areas were unreached and the Gospel spread like wildfire. Each year we saw the new believers grow by 10,000, culminating with the most in one year 33,000 souls. Today, they are still using them to reach and teach.

TCF made it possible for us to finish our Sunbeam Kids Orphanage in Cambodia. We had counted the cost to build it, but the government changed their requirements, resulting in us having to buy 1,000 square meters of land, build an office and quarantine recovery room. Soon we ran out of money, [God led] TCF to give generously with unexpected funds they received. All were finished and the children moved into beautiful homes (1 for the boys, 1 for the girls). This special place has been a safe haven for the children and a place of healing.

TCF also helped provide children's materials for the children's ministry. It literally reached thousands of children with the Gospel stories from the Bible.

In 2015 we were able to open up the Haven of Hope women's home where women who were pregnant, abused, homeless and mentally damaged, could come and stay. Most of them had considered suicide and/or abortion. They were in a safe place, learned about the Love of God, and were able to go to a good hospital for delivery. After the baby was born we worked with them to move them back into a safe society. Lives were changed and saved. One mother gave birth to a son. She left the orphanage but was planning to steal him and sell him for sex for $500. She was put out of the Haven, only to return three months later demanding [her child]. She said she could get $2,000 for him to sell him for body parts. She ran away when she was confronted. The little boy [is now] six years old and lives with the House parents who were at Haven of Hope.

Total gift from TCF 2005–2017: $216,000. Reaching into 16 Provinces.

Thank you for the opportunity to serve Him together.

Jerry and Wilma Mishler
Sunbeam Kids International

On the Frontline Ministries
Battambang, Battambang Province, Cambodia
PO Box 579210
Modesto, CA 95357

Members of these transformed churches came to know the abundant, resurrection life of Christ in the intimacy of authenticity with God and each other. This new life enabled the participants to make sense of life's experiences reclaimed as a source of spirituality and loving each other, out of which these communities impacted the world.

"Today, people are crying out for authentic communities where they can share their lives with others in a common vision, where they can find support and mutual encouragement, where they can give witness to their beliefs and work for a greater peace and justice in the world, even if they also frightened of the demands of community."[5]

Two

RESURRECTION LIVING AND GRIEF: LEARNING TO LIVE WITHOUT

> If your heart is broken, you'll find God right there;
> if you're kicked in the gut, he'll help you catch your breath.
> —Psalm 34:18 MSG

This is the story of God's work in my life and His gracious activity to bring me into a more consistent experience of living His resurrection life after significance losses.

I had closed my practice, led in dissolving the church, was no longer in ministry travel, and stopped facilitating a spiritual leadership group in Modesto. Additionally, my oldest daughter, her husband, and three of her daughters, with their husbands and kids, moved to Wyoming.

The most profound loss, Sue, my wife of fifty-nine years, died January 2, 2021. For years she had been gallantly fighting rheumatoid arthritis, which finally attacked her heart and lungs. In April 2020 she was diagnosed as having mid-stage Alzheimer's.

There were times I felt my right arm and both of my legs had been amputated, and I was trying to keep my head above the flood of emotions with only my left arm.

It was in the midst of all this loss that the resurrected Christ revealed things about Himself and me that have become life-altering

Prior to her being diagnosed, I drove her to the house of a friend, dropped her off, and returned home. When I got there, the friend called; she had forgotten her purse. I was annoyed about being inconvenienced, drove back, and gave her the purse. I was prompted to go for prayer

As I settled in, the Lord reminded me He had sent His own Son to die for His bride, the church—this divided, rebellious, "wretched, pitiful, poor, blind and naked" bride (Revelation 3:17).

I broke emotionally, weeping so hard I could hardly breathe. How dare I complain and be irritated with my precious bride when Jesus gave up so much for His? I confessed my sin. There was a major shift in my heart toward her: more present to her, more patient and understanding. I was able to quickly identify when I slid into frustration, own it, and get back to the right attitude.

Because of His reproof, this passage took on new meaning. Husbands, go all out in your love for your wives, exactly as Christ did for the church—a love marked by giving, not getting. Christ's love makes the church whole. His words evoke her beauty. Everything He does and says is designed to bring the best out of her, dressing her in dazzling white silk, radiant with holiness. And that is how husbands ought to love their wives. They're really doing themselves a favor— since they're already "one" in marriage (see Ephesians 5:25–28 MSG)

I would help her shower, get dressed, and cook the meals. It became a real joy serving her. We became more open and intimate in our relationship. As I prayed and reflected, the Lord spoke to my heart. "This is the part of My bride I love being present to and serving, the dependent and needy."

During 2021 and her death in January, God coordinated the right doctors, emergency room personnel, family support, and hospice care in such synchronicity it was jaw-dropping to everyone involved. Again He spoke to my heart.

Since I am no longer a pastor or counselor, not involved in mission activity, and now, most significant, not a husband, what am I to do and be? As I grieved all these losses, the Lord revealed that just as He had synchronized these events with Sue, He was calling me to daily be in sync with Him.

As I stay available to Him, there will be a harmonizing, a "shalom" in my walk with Him. I will still have to integrate all the losses into my life. I am to grieve authentically, incorporating these experiences in my journey. I am to take care of myself, getting the rest I need, journaling, walking, joining a grief group, taking to friends, and eating right.

Some may ask what my most significant insight so far has been. Authentic grieving means giving myself permission to scream, grovel, be angry, frustrated, cry, yell, laugh, praise God, be thankful, be confused, and sometimes all in the same hour.

It is imperative I be open to His work in coordinating my walk with Him. I am to stay present to the moment, resist past failures and future fixing, and be aware of what is happening around Him.

> If you're serious about living this new resurrection life with Christ, *act* like it. Pursue the things over which Christ presides. Don't shuffle along, eyes to the ground, absorbed with the things right in front of you. Look up, and be alert to what is going on around Christ—that's where the action is. See things from *his* perspective. (Colossians 3:1–2 MSG)

Living without Sue, I have become convicted my life has been like the hummingbird or honeybee as it flits from one flower to another extracting nectar. I can dart from one project or activity to another, wringing self-significance out of that moment. Those events can even become idolatrous, and I can perform them without God.

As I observe that's what I'm trying to do, I confess the sin. There is a freedom of not having to figure it out. If I attempt to figure those things out, I limit God's intentions, which are much larger than me trying to assign meaning or purpose to an event.

Our mind is the meaning-maker organism. To assign significance or purpose is extremely important to our understanding. However, I've come to understand that attempting to assign purpose to God's direction can lead me astray to His presence.

Lord, my heart is not proud, nor my eyes haughty;
Nor do I involve myself in great matters,
Or in things too difficult for me.

Surely I have calmed and quieted my soul;
Like a weaned child [resting] with his mother,
My soul is like a weaned child within me
[composed and freed from discontent].

O Israel, hope in the Lord
From this time forth and forever.
(Psalm 131:1–3 AMP)

All the loss has exaggerated my feelings. They're just below the surface. I can get anxious and go from one to hundred in a split second. The same goes with worry. But on the other hand, I have become extremely aware of the palpable presence of God.

A friend sent me a copy of John Wesley's prayer. One sentence in the prayer hit me so hard I was flat on my face. The sentence: "Let me be laid aside for you."

Laid aside for You? I had lost everything which gave me meaning and significance. I was no longer a husband, a father, a grandfather, a pastor, a psychologist, a ministry traveler, or group leader. Who or what am I?

The whole experience of grief was overwhelming. I wallowed in the agonizing phrase, *laid aside*, for several days. I finally saw the preposition *for*. Eventually processing through the pain, I saw the preposition, *for*.

I was staggered by the realization—to be laid aside for Jesus Christ. I was astounded: it was all gone so I could be for Him.

I confessed the sin of my self-centered anger, resentment, and unbelief. I spoke words of surrender to my Lord and yielded consciously my will to Him. Little did I realize the implications of what being laid aside for Him meant.

The Holy Spirit began convicting me of deep issues in my life grieving Him and keeping the Lord at arm's length.

I would get impatient, and the Spirit of God revealed it was a symptom of a much deeper issue. When I would pray for patients, I was attempting to deal with a symptom and not the deeper issue: I was sinning against my Father and grieving the Holy Spirit.

The truth first surfaced in my driving. I found myself being aware of how impatient I became with the drivers around me. They would cut me off, push me to go faster, or speed past to get in front of me.

In this process of exposing anger and impatience, the Holy Spirit spoke to my heart. All the time those drivers had was here on earth in this present time. They had to scratch, push, and rush to grab as much as they possibly could with the time they had. I had eternity. They had just here and now.

Moreover, being angry at them meant I was angry at God and His creation, which He paid such a high price for. As I saw my sin against God, my attitude began to change, and I have become much more rested in my driving, with a deeper understanding of what living without Christ is like for those on the road.

When I am not moving or driving in rest, I'm living in bondage.

As the Holy Spirit revealed my sin was against God, my attitude began to change in many areas.

> You're the One I've violated, and you've seen
> it all, seen the full extent of my evil.
> You have all the facts before you;
> whatever you decide about me is fair.
> I've been out of step with you for a long time,
> in the wrong since before I was born.
> What you're after is truth from the inside out.
> Enter me, then; conceive a new, true life.
> (Psalm 51:4–6 MSG)

And that broke my heart.

Being angry with others, impatient, complaining, or anxious, I was hurting my Father. After all He has done, all He has given, all He has put up with and still loved me, and now I was grieving Him! The Holy Spirit has been integrating truth into my life. My viewpoint is in the process of changing, seeing people and experiences differently.

Retired friends of mine have the finances to travel or do what they want. To be honest, I was not envious of them, but I didn't have the funds for that kind of experience.

As I reflected, I had already traveled all over the world, and

I really didn't want to travel, so what was going on with me? My retirement income provides me with a very comfortable living, though I have to watch my spending.

I was discontented. Unhappy. A malcontent.

And I was letting God know, He was not enough. Again, I broke. How could I treat my Father in such a self-centered way? As I confessed my sin against Him, there came an immediate sense of love and acceptance.

I'm in the process of learning to live on the "manna" of His presence and provision, as we shall see in Psalm 23: as we follow His presence, we have no lack,

Our brain is an anticipation organ which is persistently preparing itself for our future moments based on what happened in the past.

When I had a project to complete on appointment, I experienced a great deal of anxiety. I became aware of the fear something would stop me from getting those things done. I've felt helpless, out of control, with a sense of being harmed. I would have dreams at night of being powerless to get to some destination. It was the belief of being helpless or incapable that deeply affected my trust in God's presence.

As the Holy Spirit proceeded to show me my sin, I was overwhelmed by the impossible task of transforming the anticipatory dread. However, I came to realize God was acting as a physician, diagnosing by issue in order to heal. It was a process I had to trust. Rather than getting overwhelmed, frustrated, or defeated, I became hopeful for the healing.

I am quick to be aware of the bodily sensations of angst, tightness in my chest, and affected breathing. Spotting these reactions, identifying without judging, fixing or even figuring them out, I put them at a distance. They become powerless.

It's the old word, "Name it, and tame it."

I drive a hybrid. It has lane assist sensors, which become activated when reaching a certain speed. If I swerve, a gentle nudge on the steering wheel gets me back in lane. If I ignore it, I hear a ding. Engaging cruise control keeps me at a safe distance while traveling the freeway; it will reduce or increase speed according to the traffic.

I'm anxious when I drive on our freeways, expecting the careless or aggressive driver to cause a fatal accident. This fear is born from an anticipatory anxiety or dread that something life-threatening and dangerous is going to happen to me which I cannot predict or control.

On the way to celebrate a recent birthday eighty miles from my home, I engaged the cruise control. I made it a conscious determination not to get anxious and trust the car. I was to be aware of my apprehension and stay in the lane I was in. If the car slowed because of the car in front, wait, and when safe, change to an appropriate lane and calmly move on.

My "lane" is being present. Present to God, people, and the moment.

Rowan Williams puts it like this: "The reverence I owe to every human being is connected to the reverence I owe God, Who brings them into being and keeps them into being. I stand before holy ground when I encounter another person."[1]

The critic in my mind has been present for as long as I can remember. However, since Sue's death, self-loathing overwhelmed me. I could make the smallest mistake—drop a bottle of pills, then curse and yell how clumsy and stupid I was.

I finally turned to a photo album of my early years. There's a picture of a smiling eight-year-old boy holding a string of fish. I was with my dad at a fishing camp in New Mexico. He had put the string of fish in my hands and told me to smile. Imbedded in both my feet were pine stickers, causing them to bleed. Dad had refused to return to a stream bank where I had left my shoes. He let me know it was my fault my feet were bleeding.

His criticism affirmed what I had already come to believe: I don't do anything right, no matter how hard I try. I find myself overcompensating to do everything right and make the right decisions. I am a driven person.

As I looked at this eight-year-old, I was struck by his need to please, but also his tenacity. I broke emotionally, asking him to forgive me for my self-hate, the cursing and bitterness toward him. I thanked him for his determination, which drove me through the challenges I faced.

I went through picture after picture, asking forgiveness and expressing gratitude for his determination not to give in.

A physical sense of release moved through me. I experienced a freedom and a lifting of the burden of having to be right.

As of this writing, I am able to be kinder and more patient with myself. I still drop pills but with acceptance instead of anger. My mind is calm, less self-critical.

His resurrection work is far from being over, but I am consistently experiencing the Father's presence and a more rested state of mind and heart.

The following chapters have come out of my personal pilgrimage into community and wholeness.

Three

WISDOM, GOOD SENSE, AND SOUND JUDGMENT

Wisdom is the right use of knowledge.
—Charles Spurgeon

Do not be conformed to this world [any longer with its superficial values and customs], but be transformed *and* progressively changed [as you mature spiritually] by the renewing of your mind [focusing on godly values and ethical attitudes], so that you may prove [for yourselves] what the will of God is, that which is good and acceptable and perfect [in His plan and purpose for you].
—Romans 12:2 AMP

To be steadily transformed, to be changed, it is our choice to renew our thinking. Then we will come to know God's heart.

Dr. Gary Sibcy explains, "Spirituality is not some separate part of our functioning but refers to how well all the different components of our life work in a synchronized and coherent way. It is about how well our thinking, feeling, behaving, relating, communicating and problem solving in relationship to others and to God."[1]

I presented a workshop on how the way our mind processes information influences our spiritual formation. Afterward, a participant responded, "So it's not my lack of faith but how my mind affects my faith."

Understanding how our brain works is important in living an integrated, abundant life.

Our brain processes four hundred billion bits of information per second. We are aware of about twenty thousand each second.

Every time we learn a new fact or skill or change our behavior, we modify our brain. Our brain's ability to adapt to change and rewire itself is called plasticity. With every fresh experience, new connections are formed between neurons, and those not needed are eliminated. This reorganization of the pathways in the brain takes place at an astounding rate when we are young. The brains of adults can also be rewired, but the process take time.

It functions by transferring chemical signals between neurons causing a series of actions and reactions. This change improves short-term memory and performance.

For real modification in our thinking and behavior, there must be a long-term change in the structure of our brain. However, this takes time, practice, and struggle. The capacity to learn new truth is related to how often we participate in the new experience or truth. In fact, the greater the exertion to absorb a new fact, the more effective the learning and change in thinking and behavior.[2]

Belief and the Brain

Before you read on, how do you define faith?

Neuroscientist Andrew Newberg comments, "Having faith in the human spirit is what drives us to survive and transcend. It makes life worth living and gives meaning to life. ... Faith is embedded in our neurons and genes, and is one of the most important principles to honor in our lives."[3]

Indeed, faith is a gift from God.

> The fundamental fact of existence is that this trust in God, this faith, is the firm foundation under everything that makes life worth living. It's our handle on what we can't see. ... It's impossible to please God apart from faith. And why? Because anyone who wants to approach God must believe both that he exists *and* that he cares enough to respond to those who seek him. (Hebrews 11:1, 6 MSG)

Faith brings into existence that which is in the unseen spiritual dimension and has the confidence God will bring to fulfillment.

Faith is a choice to be committed to that which is beyond us, which gives us significance and meaning. It is an allegiance or loyalty, a faithfulness of a subordinate to a superior or a group or cause.

Our brain's nerve cells' firing patterns are influenced by past incidents, which hampers openness, adaptability, and a balanced state of mind.

In other words, our allegiance or belief system is affected by previous incidents, which influence how our brain processes present experiences. The beliefs we assume are affected by primary neurological firing patterns shaped by past events.

I was praying with a group of guys from our church concerning the start-up of a counseling service, Sonburst. As they prayed, I cringed in absolute terror. I was convinced God was setting me up for failure. He was going to expose me as being stupid for trusting Him. I screamed at Him to leave me alone.

The men piled on top of me, weeping and praying for me. For years I had been a cynic regarding God when it came to me or our family. I would berate God, feeling they were treated unfairly, rejected, or hurt emotionally. The skepticism was an ingrained pattern of response which became so painful it was here with these loving guys that I began to deal with it.

At that moment I became aware of the Lord whispering, "Now you see I am not your dad you could not trust. I am your heavenly Father who will show you My faithfulness." That night I realized there was an implicit or buried memory. My dad made all kind of promises and never followed through. Time after time I would trust him, and he would disappoint me. Eventually I swore I would not trust him and leave me feeling foolish.

Within six months of establishing the center I had a full client schedule.

Because the pattern was so deep, it took some time for me to label the knee-jerk reaction and own it as a thought.

I will remind myself to reframe the situation by telling my Father I was looking forward to how He would handle it and be open to join in with Him when called to do so. In other words, put my confidence in Him for the best outcome.

I want to be clear here. I finally came to the place of not blaming my dad. I realized I am responsible for how I allowed him to influence my perception and therefore my belief about God and others. I had to let go of my expectations of him. I also had to let go of the anger, forgive him, and ultimately acknowledge what he was, as a man in bondage to alcohol. I can say I love him just as he is without approving what he does.

Can we honestly own the thinking patterns keeping us from

knowing something greater, something beyond those patterns, a loving Lord seeking to love us into wholeness? The question is are we willing to be open to the possibility there is an active God lovingly in control in the midst of life's inexplicable challenges?

Reflect on a past situation you were unable to remedy. What were your feelings? What negative thoughts did you have about yourself? Does the self-concept from that time define all you are? To what extent does it affect your trust in God?

James Fowler ponders the following: (I suggest you take time with each question, it will be helpful to write down your thoughts.)

What are you spending your life for? What commands and receives your best times and energy?

What causes, dreams, goals, and institutions are you pouring out your life for?

As you live your life, what power or powers do you fear or dread? What power or powers do you rely on and trust?

To what or whom do you rely on and trust?

To what or whom are you committed in life? In death?

With whom or what group do you share your most sacred and private hopes for your life and for the lives of those you love?

What are the most sacred hopes, the most compelling goals and purposes in your life?[4]

What claims your best times? What powers do you rely on or trust? When circumstances fall apart and possibilities die, what do you count on? Where do you find significance or meaning?

Life-Insight: Joe

He was a young, talented baseball player. Matter of fact, he was playing in the minor leagues, there with the potential of playing in the majors. He depended upon and had faith in his ability to succeed. He was committed to working hard, practicing hard, pushing himself. This was worth spending his life for, his best times dreamed of—he could go on to play in the majors.

Two things took place: when the season was over, he had nothing to live for, and after four years he was going no place. He walked away from that life.

Now what choices was he going to make? Where was he going to put his allegiance? What was he going to spend his life for? What dreams or goals was he going to be committed to? What powers was he going to depend upon?

These were the issues he wrestled with. As he floundered in his mind, Lauren, his wife, shared her newfound faith in Christ. Stumbling through doubt and questions, Joe came to realize this Christ was going to be the unifying factor for his life. Now he has become a businessman with an authentic dependency on God as he impacts his workaday world. As former president of a company, he took daily walks to see how his eighty-plus employees were doing. They felt free to come to his office to pray, get advice on finances, and seek his wisdom on family relationships.

The Brain and Old Patterns

Newberg and Waldman explain we have two neurological wolves in our brain. The older one crouches in the limbic system with anger and fear. This wolf is fast and proficient and can be lethal. A younger wolf shelters in the frontal lobe and anterior cingulate. Its personality is ruled by compassion, reason, empathy, and logic. This younger wolf is playful and creative yet susceptible and slower to react than the older, more emotional wolf.[5]

Recently I received a subpoena from an attorney for the defense concerning the defendant's sexual abuse of my client.

Their intention was to question my diagnosis, treatment plan, and prognosis. Even though I knew they had no legal means to do so, I was frozen with fear. The rational part of my brain could not even process that reality. The old wolf was on a rampage of emotional upheaval.

Of course I did not have to testify.

I finally realized I reacted in the belief I was not able to protect my client. My "turf" in our family was to protect my mom from my violent and unpredictable dad. The old wolf was toothless. I was powerless to take care of my client. Further, I would be exposed as not knowing what I was talking about, a fraud.

Dr. Tim Jennings submits, "We have the power to choose what to believe, but what we believe has power over us, power to heal or power to destroy."[6]

So, which wolf makes grownup moral decisions? It depends on which one we feed. When we give way to emotions, the older wolves run unbridled, and we restrain the younger wolves from their logical and compassionate response.

How do you feed the young wolves? By choosing to stand back and reflect on a strained relationship, rather than be swept away by the feelings. The power to direct your attention has with it the power to shape your brain's firing pattern.

It's a process of disengagement, of liberating yourself from those situations that ensnare your emotions. It is not indifference or denial but simply being present to the circumstance, with the ability to view what is going on without trying to criticize or correct at that moment.

The 1957 Plymouth has high fender taillights and a pushbutton transmission. Among its technological wonders, button-sized lights on the dashboard turn red to let you know if the oil or water is low. These are called "idiot lights."

I don't yell at the lights (unless I'm in a bad mood, of course). I check the oil or water and take necessary steps to address the issue.

Looking at the light on the dashboard is a way of being disengaged about stressful places in our life.

When there are patterns of red lights turning on, it can be an indication of thinking processes keeping us in bondage.

The Holy Spirit within us as Reality Seeker works to reveal the central driving force of our life, the heart. It is what defines us and motivates us.

> The heart is hopelessly dark and deceitful,
>> a puzzle that no one can figure out.
> But I, GOD, search the heart
>> and examine the mind.
> I get to the heart of the human.
> I get to the root of things.
> I treat them as they really are,
>> not as they pretend to be.
> (Jeremiah 17:9–10 MSG)

Reflect on a recent or significant stressful setting. What is the light on the dashboard revealing about your thoughts or feelings?

Accept the emotions to be what they are. What the thoughts and feelings that surface as you sit back and are aware of the red light? What are your thoughts about God?

When we are disengaged, we accept things as they are without judging them. The thought and feeling are not facts of who we are. They give us a detachment to the event.

Observation is a necessary capacity because we can sense what is happening from a detached distance. It allows ourselves some space in which to become more adaptable. We can join in fully without being swept up in the immediate reactions we may have.[7]

Eric Berne wrote, "Awareness requires living in the here and now, and not in the elsewhere, the past or the future."[8]

The Brain and Shame

> When the woman saw that the fruit of the tree was good for food and pleasing to the eye, and also desirable for gaining wisdom, she took some and ate it. She also gave some to her husband, who was with her, and he ate it. Then the eyes of both of them were opened, and they realized they were naked; so they sewed fig leaves together and made coverings for themselves.
>
> Then the man and his wife heard the sound of the LORD God as he was walking in the garden in the cool of the day, and they hid from the LORD God among the trees of the garden. But the LORD God called to the man, "Where are you?"
>
> He answered, "I heard you in the garden, and I was afraid because I was naked; so I hid." (Genesis 3:6–10)

Shame is more than the loss of face or embarrassment. Shame is the inner sense of being completely diminished as a person. Shame is the self, judging the self. A moment of shame may be humiliation so painful or an indignity so profound that one feels one has been robbed of his or her dignity or exposed as basically inadequate, bad, or worthy of rejection. A pervasive sense of shame is the ongoing premise that one is fundamentally bad, inadequate, defective, unworthy, or not fully valid as a human being.[9]

Underline the words that personally resonate with you. You will be using the underlined words later.

Shame is a perversion of humility.

Life-Insight: Miriam

The Jews for Jesus invited me to be their chaplain during their "Behold Our God" campaign in Cape Town, South Africa. I was to lead the chapel service, be available to counsel, and head the on-site intercession team from our church as they presented Christ as Messiah to the thousands of Jews coming there during Christmas

Miriam confessed she was intimidated by others in the group. She shamefully professed she was not as passionate as Suzan, not as smart as Hannah, not as knowledgeable as Deborah. She was considering returning to Austria.

I asked, what if God wanted her "not as," just to be who she was where she was? Was she open not to be as passionate as Suzan, not as smart as Hannah, not as knowledgeable as Deborah? Could she believe Messiah would use her just the way she was?

That got her attention. For her it was an epiphany, a moment of sudden insight; in her pain, she was heart-ready to receive.

She identified, without self-judgment, her "not-as-good-as thinking." In prayer, she expressed gratitude for the gift she was to the group and the campaign. She was not frightened by the reactions of the visiting Jews.

What secret was provoking Miriam's shame? What insightful truth freed her?

In what circumstances do you compare yourself with others? Write it down. What words in the definition of shame apply to you there? In what way do those words shape how you think about God?

There are clusters of cell-firing patterns in our brain which affect our belief, feelings, and behavior regarding our life. They distort our perceptions and create perspectives of ourselves, God, and others. Like a thermostat in the room, these states turn on without our being aware of their influence. So it is with shame: we protect ourselves from being known.

Subterranean shame drives us to succeed and prove to ourselves we are worthy and valuable. It can motivate us to avoid being close. A felt sense of failure can trigger the sense of being damaged goods. We then will react, keeping distant from the ones nearest us.

As with Adam, fear driven by shame causes us to cover ourselves. We hide from the most meaningful relationships in our life because we are fearful of being exposed. We sew fig leaves, covering our humiliation with leaves of busyness, success, or achievement.

The power of shame comes from keeping secrets. When God called Adam to come from behind the tree, He was identifying the power of secrecy that goaded Adam there.

Earlier in this Psalm, David extols God for His precious thoughts. It is in this trust he prays:

> Investigate my life, O God,
>> find out everything about me;
> Cross-examine and test me,
>> get a clear picture of what I'm about;
> See for yourself whether I've done anything wrong—
>> then guide me on the road to eternal life.
> (Psalm 139:23–24 MSG)

In these situations our heavenly Father is searching and examining our responses, not to reprimand but to release us from the lies we believe.

One way we can join with God in uncovering and confront shame is using Daniel Amen and Automatic Negative Thinking suggestions.

Using the underlined words in the previous definition of shame, in what situation or relationships are you most aware of those feelings? Be free to stand back and note the situation. Don't overanalyze, just be present. What do you notice? Don't try to fix.

What is the specific negative thought you believe about yourself. The negative though or negative cognation is important to identify.

Is that thought 100 percent true? Yes or no.

What do I feel like and act like when I believe that negative thought?

What would I feel like and act like if I did not believe that negative thought?

What is the direct opposite of the negative thought?

Which is most true?[10]

(I have personally added this question: Now, what does the Lord think of you?)

Life-Insight: Lizzy

Her self-revealing honesty catches you off guard like an avalanche burying you upside down. Lizzy, in language which cannot be printed here, scoffs, "These mothers whose life is their kids, it makes me puke. I feel terrible; mine drive me crazy. I can't wait for their father to take them off my hands. What's wrong with me?"

Lizzy realized her kids, who drove her crazy, were a reflection of how she perceived herself. She saw herself as an intrusion, a pain to others. As a child she was constantly told she was too much, a bother. And it created a schema, a way she perceived life and those around her. Like a thermostat turning on the heater in a cold room, the pressure of raising four children without a mate created the "perfect storm" of self-hatred.

So here's how she began to deal with the Automatic Negative Thoughts.

As Lizzy reflected on her thoughts about her kids being such an intrusive pain, she wrote out and shared the following thought process:

What specific negative thought are you believing about yourself?

"I can't wait for my kids to get out of my hair. I am a terrible mother. A failure."

Is that thought 100 percent true?

"No, I am not always a failure with my kids."

What do I act like and feel like when I believe I am a failure?

"Angry at myself, my kids and my ex. Hopeless and closed off to God."

What would I feel like and act like if I did not believe I was a failure?'

"I would be more present with my kids and be happier with myself."

What is the direct opposite of believing I am a failure?

"I am a capable mom who loves her children."

What is most true?

"I am in the process of being the capable mom God created me to be."

Now, what does the Lord think of you?

"He loves and values me even when I feel like a bother or have negative feelings about my kids."

Lizzy had to continue to work with this process until it became a truth lived out in her life. She has become more present with her children, being less anxious or angry. We also worked together on how to take time for herself to recharge.

Shame distorts authentic humility, creating condemnation rather than Holy Spirit conviction.

Conviction reveals our sin in order to correct without humiliation. Conviction brings freedom as we confess. Conviction deals with specific offenses without attacking our entire personality. It frees us to move on without being stuck. It opens us to be closer to God and each other rather than withdrawing from God and others.

Appendix A is a list of Negative Perceptions, which can help you to identify the negative beliefs.

Whenever we conceive ourselves in the self-judgment of "What's wrong with me?" we inhibit the Holy Spirit, the Spirit of Truth, from revealing what the Lord has to say about us.

If you choose to work with this process, it will take some time and practice, and in some cases, you'll have to push through the steps until consistent change is realized.

It may be helpful to find a friend you can talk to as you work these steps.

The Brain and Relationships

Outside in our patio, attached to a large beam is a delicate wind chime. Its balance has been created by a craftsman to respond to the slightest breeze. It speaks to me concerning my relationships. One side of the chime is me; the opposite side, others; and the apex connected to the beam, God. The breeze, the Holy Spirit.

As the triune God is in perfect communion and balance within Himself, He created us to be an expression of that reality in relationships, flowing in the freedom in His Spirit. The problems we have in connecting with others reveal we are also out of balance with God.

> Then God said, "Let us make mankind in our image, in our likeness, so that they may rule over the fish in the sea and the birds in the sky, over the livestock and all the wild animals, and over all the creatures that move along the ground."
> So God created mankind in his own image,
> in the image of God he created them;
> male and female he created them. (Genesis 1:26–27)

Kingdom as the reign of Christ in Relationships

As I work with couples as clients, I want them to understand that how they treat each other uncovers what their relationship with God is like.

Linda Graham expounds, "Relating to one another, one on one, couples, families, or in larger social groups, is the most complex thing human beings do, more complex than writing a symphony or running a government or solving global warming."[11]

Life-Insight: Bobbie

Not knowing what do, her marriage in trouble, Bobbie began the painful journey of self- discovery and learning to face what the pain said to her. She eventually saw that the patterns of relationships she established had everything to do with how her mind processed those interactions. These configurations impacted what she believed about God, His Word, and His world.

Able to shop only at bargain clothing stores, she could not bring herself to shop in upscale stores in San Francisco. More than being fearful of the drive, more than trying not to upset her husband, she believed she was only worth cheap clothes.

She had the money, not the belief.

Do for others, not for self.

She still must bear the load: her husband, off being successful in other places; a son dead in an auto accident; another in bondage to drugs; having custody of a granddaughter.

Starting to trust that perhaps she was of worth because God cared for her, she could go to the big city. Perhaps she could take some control of her life without giving so much of her self away.

I asked her to sort out how she was reacting to the expectations of those closest to her—not to analyze, judge, or fix. Just to be open to what she was thinking in those transactions, what she was feeling. Just to be present to herself.

She struggled with the process. It was so new. Before, she would be harsh in self-judgment, ending up angry not only at herself but at others. She was continuing to carry the hurt, the burden.

She began see she was primed to scan for the perceived danger of rejection by the alarm bell in her mind. As she continued the work in counseling, she was able to identify the "mind thing" and move on.

Also, as she flourished in being valued by God, she cognitively, experience by experience, decided to trust Him. She discovered that having to take care of herself as a child meant she could not trust others to do so. This belief was a construct that influenced how she perceived God.

Finally she begins by asking her busy, successful husband to follow through on promises he had made regarding the backlog of problems with the house, letting him know she would get the work hired out if he was too busy.

He promised but could never follow through; instead, he traveled. She hired to have the work done. He protested. She smiled. New garage door, her office, new roof, windows, his private home office, and a new kitchen—he loves it all.

Understanding how her mind processed relationships, as she shared in a safe environment, her trust in God grew, and she became more connected with Christ. And in the process of learning that her life now was a stewardship to God, saying no to others was an obedience to her Lord. Bobbie is now much more open and less rigid working with all her challenges. She sees her husband in a clearer light and is able to relate to him more authentically.

As the Holy Spirit continued to entice her to be more Christlike, she "laid down her life" before the Lord in the course of letting go of the fear of rejection by her husband and others. Through this process she has become the "door" by which her family can choose to enter and participate in God's activity.

How do you respond to Bobbie's story? Are there places you can identify with her? How do you see faith operating in her situation and yours?

Are there relationships, situations, or systems in which you have allowed your life to be taken from you? What has been your reaction? What would be the most challenging if you began to take your life back?

> This is why the Father loves me: because I freely lay down my life. And so I am free to take it up again. No one takes it from me. I lay it down of my own free will. I have the right to lay it down; I also have

the right to take it up again. I received this authority personally from my Father. (John 10:17–18 MSG)

When there is a pattern of freezing or feeling invisible, researchers have found that unresolved loss in the caregiver tended to create a sense of disoriented attachment in their infant, especially when the caregiver had also experienced an unresolved trauma prior to the loss. It reveals a disruption or flooding of the attachment system by overwhelming fear, resulting in a feeling of freezing and/ or dissociation—a sense of being disconnected from reality. This reaction is the ultimate self-protection system.[12]

Christlike Communicating

Do nothing out of selfish ambition or vain conceit. Rather, in humility value others above yourselves, not looking to your own interests but each of you to the interests of the others.

In your relationships with one another, have the same mindset as Christ Jesus:

> Who, being in very nature God,
>   did not consider equality with God?
> Something to be used to his own advantage;
> Rather, he made himself nothing
>   by taking the very nature of a servant,
>   being made in human likeness.
> And being found in appearance as a man,
>   he humbled himself
>   by becoming obedient to death— even death
>   on a cross!

Therefore God exalted him to the highest place
and gave him the name that is above every
name,
That at the name of Jesus every knee should bow,
in heaven and on earth and under the earth,
And every tongue acknowledge that Jesus Christ
is Lord,
to the glory of God the Father.
(Philippians 2:3–11)

This is a significant statement regarding interpersonal relationships: valuing others above ourselves. It demands Christlike thinking.

He had to let go of His entitlement. In embracing servanthood, He was truly human and became obedient to the cross and is now revealed as Lord of lords.

As a communication coach with families, I lead them to understand Christlike listening requires a process of letting go of perceived entitlements or holding on to bitterness, anger, or demands; becoming servants to each by putting themselves in the other's mindset; and dying to their defenses of explanations, excuses, and denials. In this relational process, Christ's lordship is realized.

In transaction with others we can find ourselves being defensive rather than setting aside our rights. We are to set aside our explanations, defenses, and judgments and seek to listen beyond the words to the heart.

Reflect on the situations that may stimulate defensive reactions from you. What do you observe? Can you work behind to the thinking that drives your reaction? If so what is it?

Or how do you react to those who are defensive toward you?

With whom or what do you need to change? What would happen if you did?

Life-Insight: Piper and Frank

Married for more than twenty-five years, they had given up to an unfulfilled life together. Their mutual commitment to Christ created a self-regard in each which drove them to "hang in there," even though unfulfilled. The support of the pastoral staff and previous counseling experiences offered little hope—even creating further despair, a living death. Their defense mechanisms created a power conflict so extensive they eventually resigned themselves to a life of mutual disconnection.

Compelled by their dedication to Christ, they began the arduous exploration of learning how to genuinely listen to each other's heart. They discovered the unconscious lies each bought into, creating self-protective barriers to intimacy. Eventually expressing and experiencing forgiveness, each began to acknowledge a mutual respect and love for the other's faith expression—how each lived out their commitment to Christ.

Work and growth continues, and they are discovering life in Christ and with each other. They still have issues; however, they are now able to talk about and resolve them.

Of the relationships you find yourself in, which has affected your freedom in Christ? Are there patterns God uses to reveal how self-protective you are? Perhaps defensive? Are you becoming aware of the unconscious lies creating walls between you, God, and those relationships?

Four

ATTENDING: BEING PRESENT WITH OR AWARE OF ANOTHER

> Attention is the beginning of devotion.
> —Mary Oliver

> Step out of the traffic! Take a long,
> loving look at me, your High God,
> above politics, above everything.
> —Psalm 46:10 MSG

In offering admiration to something or someone outside us, gratitude enables us to interact with something not only larger than ourselves but also profoundly worthy and encouraging. It opens our eyes to the wonder of life, something to admire, delight in, and rejoice in. In this process be open to the vibrant, resurrection life of Christ flowing though us.

Dr. Timothy Jennings has found that daily reflecting on the goodness of God significantly improved the lives of those who did so twelve minutes a day for thirty days. The participants, sixty-five years old or older, had better memory, lower blood pressure, and clearer thinking reflecting on the love of God. Brain research has demonstrated the kind of God you worship changes your brain. Only the worship of the God of love brings about healing.[1]

The reason:

> If you contemplate God long enough, something surprising happens in the brain. Neural functioning begins to change. Different circuits become activated, while others become deactivated. New dendrites are formed, and new synaptic connections are made, and the brain becomes more sensitive to subtle realms of experience. Perceptions also alter, beliefs began to change, and if God has meeting for you, then God becomes neurologically real. For some, God may remain a primitive concept, limited to the way a child interprets the world. But for most people, God is transformed into a symbol or metaphor experiencing a wide range of personal, ethical, social, and universal values.[2]

As you move through your day, using the following scriptures, reflect on a word in the verse, think about synonyms that come to mind and how it affects your world. Consider ways in which He has come to you in the words you are mulling over. Are there people around you who have displayed these attributes? With the words in mind, thank Him for how He has come to you during your day and in those you have encountered.

When your mind wanders, that's okay; just bring your thoughts back to the moment. Over time your thinking will change. Seasoned hikers will explain when they find themselves off the path, they turn around and retrace their steps back to where they went astray.

Also, remember, when we give intentional, focused attention to a thought, our brain then fires differently: it changes with experience, which activates neural firing and eventually affects its very structure. This system, known as Hebbian learning—"cells that fire together, wire together"—is the basic way all organisms gain new knowledge about the world.[3]

Furthermore, it will take time to draw your driven, busy day into His presence. Just begin where you are, and relinquish the struggle of where you think you ought to be.

If this is new for you, start with a short period—say, about two minutes a day. Keep it simple. Don't attempt too much at first. If you can read the scripture and praise Him for one thing, just do that. It may take a week or a month. You will begin to feel more comfortable and drawn to do four minutes and so on.

You may want to dwell on each word in this verse for several days. You are on a journey and do not have to hurry through these words of truth. Or you may want to move on to the next site. This is not a memory exercise. So be patient with yourself in this process. Give your thinking process time to change.

> I love you, LORD, my strength.
> The LORD is my rock, my fortress and my deliverer;
>   my God is my rock, in whom I take refuge,
>   my shield and the horn of my salvation, my
>   stronghold.
> (Psalm 18:1–2)

Imagine Christ is sitting with you as you speak with Him. In what ways would you express your love to Him? What does it mean to you personally that He is your "strength; [You, Lord, are] my rock, my fortress and my deliverer; my God is my rock, in whom I take refuge, my shield and the horn of my salvation, my stronghold"?

Simply put, to praise is to adore Him for who He is, and to give thanks is to be grateful for what He has done

I have presented several scriptures for your thoughts.

> You, Lord, are forgiving and good,
>> abounding in love to all who call to you. (Psalm 86:5)

> The LORD is gracious and righteous;
>> our God is full of compassion. (Psalm 116:5)

> I know that the LORD secures justice for the poor
>> and upholds the cause of the needy.
>> (Psalm 140:12)

Let us fix our eyes on Jesus, the author, and perfector of faith, who for the joy set before him he endured the cross, scorning its shame, and sat down at the right hand of the throne of God. (Hebrews 12:2)

To the angel of the church in Smyrna write:
> These are the words of him who is the First and the Last, who died and came to life again. (Revelation 2:8)

To the angel of the church in Laodicea write:
> These are the words of the Amen, the faithful and true witness, the ruler of God's creation. (Revelation 3:14)

I, Jesus, have sent my angel to give you this testimony for the churches. I am the Root and the Offspring of David, and the bright Morning Star. (Revelation 22:16)

I am the Bread of Life. (John 6:48 MSG)

Both the one who makes people holy and those who are made holy are of the same family. So Jesus is not ashamed to call them brothers and sisters. (Hebrews 2:11)

For to us a child is born,
  to us a son is given,
  and the government will be on his shoulders.
And he will be called
  Wonderful Counselor, Mighty God,
  Everlasting Father, Prince of Peace. (Isaiah 9:6)

The deliverer will come from Zion;
he will turn godlessness away from Jacob.
(Romans 11:26)

Therefore Jesus said again, "Very truly I tell you, I am the gate for the sheep." (John 10:7)

The virgin will conceive and give birth to a son, and they will call him Immanuel (which means "God with us"). (Matthew 1:23)

On that day a fountain will be opened to the house of David and the inhabitants of Jerusalem, to cleanse them from sin and impurity. (Zechariah 13:1)

There is one God and one mediator between God and mankind, the man Christ Jesus. (1 Timothy 2:5)

[Jesus] gave himself as a ransom for all people. This has now been witnessed to at the proper time. (1 Timothy 2:6)

You killed the author of life, but God raised him from the dead. We are witnesses of this. (Acts 3:15)

He is the atoning sacrifice for our sins, and not only for ours but also for the sins of the whole world. (1 John 2:2)

Christ loved us and gave himself up for us as a fragrant offering and sacrifice to God. (Ephesians 5:2)

To the angel of the church in Philadelphia write:
These are the words of him who is holy and true, who holds the key of David. What he opens no one can shut, and what he shuts no one can open. (Revelation 3:7)

Sovereign Lord, as you have promised,
you may now dismiss your servant in peace.
For my eyes have seen your salvation.
(Luke 2:29–30)

For you who revere my name, the sun of righteousness will rise with healing in its rays. And you will go out and frolic like well-fed calves. (Malachi 4:2)

My dear children, I write this to you so that you will not sin. But if anybody does sin, we have an advocate with the Father—Jesus Christ, the Righteous One. (1 John 2:1)

Whoever does not love does not know God, because God is love. This is how God showed his love among us: He sent his one and only Son into the world that we might live through him. (1 John 4:8–9)

Oh, the depth of the riches of the wisdom and knowledge of God!
How unsearchable his judgments,
and his paths beyond tracing out!
(Rom. 11:33)

God also said to Moses, "Say to the Israelites, 'The LORD, the God of your fathers—the God of Abraham, the God of Isaac and the God of Jacob— has sent me to you.'
"This is my name forever,
the name you shall call me
from generation to generation."
(Exodus 3:15)

In the beginning you laid the foundations of the earth,
and the heavens are the work of your hands …
But you remain the same,
and your years will never end.
(Psalm 102:25, 27)

Reflect through each word in the following scripture, which describes Christ and His work.

> We look at this Son and see the God who cannot be seen. We look at this Son and see God's original purpose in everything created. For everything, absolutely everything, above and below, visible and invisible, rank after rank after rank of angels— *everything* got started in him and finds its purpose in him. He was there before any of it came into existence and holds it all together right up to this moment. And when it comes to the church, he organizes and holds it together, like a head does a body.
>
> He was supreme in the beginning and—leading the resurrection parade—he is supreme in the end. From beginning to end he's there, towering far above everything, everyone. So spacious is he, so roomy, that everything of God finds its proper place in him without crowding. Not only that, but all the broken and dislocated pieces of the universe—people and things, animals and atoms—get properly fixed and fit together in vibrant harmonies, all because of his death, his blood that poured down from the cross. (Colossians 1:15–20 MSG)

Appendix B gives a link to all the names of Christ if you want to continue beyond what is provided here.

You might want to work through the Psalms and the words there describing the Lord. "The One enthroned in heaven"—what comes to your mind as you process that name? What way has He shown Himself in that way?

I encourage you to praise and thank Him when you receive income and pay your bills. Put a sticky-note reminder in your checkbook or on your computer if you use the internet.

Try this experiment for a week: thank or praise Him for five different things every day. When you shower, get dressed, eat breakfast, or get involved in the activities of the day, thank or praise Him for five things involved in getting those things done. Sounds silly, but it will improve your thinking as you go through the day. Just try it for a week.

There is evidence such exercises can change thinking patterns in our brain and positively influence our well-being because we do so with intention. Moreover, we become more adjusted to His loving presence and aware of His gifts to us, no matter how small.

If you forget, that's okay. Start with the place where you remembered to do so.

What if I don't feel grateful or want to praise Him?

Even if you don't feel like thanking or praising Him, do it anyway. You are acting in faith, not feeling. Admit it to the Lord, and go ahead and thank or praise Him anyhow!

Life-Insight: Victoria

She was a child of God, wanting to know Him deeply. In her family she had to be the strong one as a child.

She had two problems: she desired to know Christ, and she had to be tough in order to be valued. She had come to the end of herself—no longer resilient, and angry at her own emotional weakness to help her children facing life's problems.

I challenged her to praise God anyhow. She really got mad, not at herself, but me. "That's stupid," she spat.

"Yep," says I.

"Doesn't make sense"

"Yep."

"I'm *not* going to do it." Heels dug in.

"I don't care. Do it anyway."

"I don't believe it." Arms crossed.

"I don't care. Do it anyway."

"That's stupid."

"You've already said that."

Grumbling," Will you help me?"

"No, you're a big girl. Anyway, you will do this for the next week, and I'm not on call to aid you."

Arms crossed, crossed at me, crossed at God, she started to let Him know what she thought of this "stupid" idea. She didn't believe what she would be saying, and so on.

"You've whined enough; get on with it."

Stumbling, she began to thank and praise God for who He was and His loving acts, and she was too exhausted to be of real support for her children.

"So there, are you satisfied?"

"Yep."

Next week. "I told Lynn [her husband] and he just snickered. I kept whining and stayed with the praise about being helpless. All is not changed, but I now see how I was letting my emotions dictate my relationship with Christ."

"Good. See you next week."

"Is that all?"

"Yep."

We continued to work with her regarding praise and thankfulness and issues regarding her children. Eventually Victoria began to possess joy and a sense of well-being. Her perception of being weak changed. She was more relaxed when it came to problems with her grown children. She understood that "not fixing" displayed not helplessness but a trust in God.

You will find that daring gratitude and bold praise affect your thinking. So stay at it in your muddled, dark place. Christ will eventually reveal Himself to you. Audacious praise and thanksgiving about God's qualities in an unjust or challenging situation can create confusing and ambivalent emotions; do not give up.

The capacity to value and see the blessings of our life rather than allowing our burden to define us is essential to authentic happiness.

When God gives us less than we expect, could it be He is developing gratitude? As He provided manna in the wilderness, He is creating dependence on Him.

I encourage you to keep a gratitude journal. The spiritual, emotional, and physical effects can be amazing. See Appendix C: How to Create a Gratitude Journal.

If you want to strengthen your time of personal worship, Appendix D: Enhancing Personal Worship can help.

Five

MUSINGS: A TIME OF REFLECTION OR THOUGHT

> Reflective thinking turns experience into insight.
> —John C. Maxwell

Trinity Baptist Church, Corpus Christi, Texas. There she was, black dress, black scarf, large brown eyes, wearing Avon, "Here's My Heart." Her name: Sue. I'm in trouble—smitten by her beauty. And *that* perfume ... *wow!*

The next few days I became a stalker. Any girl on campus wearing *that* perfume I would follow sniffing, enthralled. The slightest whiff of *that* perfume reminded me of her. The slimmest hint of *that* perfume nudged me into Sue's presence.

As you began this part of our journey, I pray you will find yourself easily nudged into an awareness of the One who created you.

It can take time to learn how to draw your driven, busy day into His presence. Just began where you are, and relinquish the struggle of where you think you ought to be.

Through our work with individuals and small groups, we have come to advise, if a scripture, thought, or question "speaks" to you, pause to reflect on it rather than moving on, as you might do in a daily devotional.

The scriptures, questions, and insights are designed to create a more consistent, open connectedness as you meet Christ though reflection and experience the dynamic resurrection presence of Christ.

I repeat questions in the context of different scriptures with various applications. This is intentional. Encountering diverse passages with these reflections may stimulate new insight. Remember, learning a new truth takes practice.

Slowly read through the scripture, pondering the deeper meaning, as if you were present to the event, relating to the material as a personal encounter rather than an intellectual exercise.

Appendix E, Small Group Leader's Guide, gives guidelines for using the following in small groups.

Guided by Grace – Psalm 23

Psalm 23 rests between the Psalm of the cross, "My God, my God, why have you forsaken me? Why are you so far from saving me, so far from my cries of anguish?" (22:1), and the Psalm of His return, "Lift up your heads, you gates; be lifted up, you ancient doors, that the King of glory may come in. Who is this King of glory? The LORD strong and mighty, the LORD mighty in battle" (24:7–8). However, the best-known utterance of David, number 23, is the Psalm of His presence: God guiding His flock by grace. My working definition of grace: "It's too good to be true, but it is."

During coffee Dr. J. Harold Smith shared with us the following story. He was touring the Hebron Valley when he noticed shepherds leading their flock to a watering hole. Intriguingly, both flocks intermingled to the point he could not tell one flock from the other. He asked the guide, how could either shepherd retrieve his own flock without losing one of his own? The guide told him to wait until the flocks were watered.

After some time, one shepherd started to call out to his flock. Each of the owner's sheep moved out with him. The guide explained they knew the shepherd and his voice.

Another shepherd appeared on the scene, not guiding but driving his flock. J. Harold asked his guide about the difference, and he was told they were being driven to slaughter.

Take a moment before reading, and put yourself in David's place. Let the story be yours. Be aware of the Shepherd's voice as He draws you to Himself in His grace.

> The LORD is my Shepherd [to feed, to guide and to
> shield me],
> > I shall not want. (Psalm 23:1 AMP)

As we are living in the "now-ness" of His presence, the Lord is passionate to shepherd us so we will lack nothing and bring honor to Him and His care.

Pardon my pickiness. All the verbs in this psalm are in a tense which means a present ongoing-ness. For example, in verse 1. "YAHWEH one-being-shepherd-of –me" (participle: expresses verbal action) is the literal translation. Or "not I shall-be-lack" (imperfect: in the Hebrew the imperfect generally describes actions not completed which occur in the present or the future). Or in verse 2, "he-is-making-reclining-me" (imperfect).

So what's the point of my pickiness? Think with me: could it be that I am "living in lack" because I am not open in the present moment to "YAHWEH (the "I AM") one-being-shepherd-of-me?"

This is what this Psalm is about, faith-living in the "right-now-ness" of God's gracious presence, care, and provision. It is a description of His shepherding commitment.

His presence defines our needs. Outside His presence, our need defines us.

The fracture created by Adam brought about an imbalance in all the world's systems—environmental, ecological, political, social, and personal. In this rupture all of us have unfulfilled needs, which creates a spirit of entitlement, bitterness, resentment, or envy.

This is because our lower brain is consumed with our perceived survival, and we can go to any extent to secure our needs. We are responsible to identify this process and bring that thinking in line with Christ. Our deficiency can personify us as we attempt to address our unsatisfied wants on our own.

These issues are symptoms of a deeper problem: we refuse to stay in the moment where His I AM resides. We snub God, not relying on Him to supply our needs in His way and timing.

To be significant—to have meaning within ourselves and others—is a basic, legitimate need. However, shame can distort significance into egocentric expectations of how others see us. And it is what we value.

Guided by Grace

> "The LORD is my Shepherd [to feed, to guide and
> to shield me], I shall not want" (Psalm 23:1 (AMP).

Because our lower brain is consumed with our survival, we will go to any extent to secure our unmet needs or desires. We are responsible to identify these drives and bring that thinking in line with Christ.

Our deficiency keeps us in bondage we attempt to address these discontented areas on our own.

These issues are symptoms of a deeper problem: we refuse to stay in the moment where His I AM resides. We snub God, not relying on Him to supply our needs in His way and timing.

Think about those places of discontent or "not enough-ness" in your relationships or situations, and observe your reaction. What are your feelings?

How has that affected your relationship to God? To others? What is hindering you from resting in His presence and provision there?

"He lets me lie down in green pastures" (23:2 AMP).

In increase of vegetation, He is causing us to stretch out. We can lie down when we are free from fear, tension, aggravation, and hunger to ruminate, to ponder His attentive care.

Sheep ruminate, a verb that means "to chew again," They will eat quickly and allow saliva to mix with the foliage. Later, regurgitated, it is chewed and then swallowed. In David's picture, the sheep chew their cud lying down. The Shepherd by His very presence has established an environment of peace and provision.

Are you aware of the unfulfilled needs impacting your relationship to God and others? What are they? In what way do they shape your life?

"He leads me beside the still *and* quiet waters" (Psalm 23:2 AMP).

He guides us to clear, pure, restful waters so we can drink to give us strength, vitality and health.

So often our discontent drives us to contaminated waters polluting our hearts, our thoughts which we are not aware of. This is like drinking poison, thinking it will heal us. Bitterness, unforgiveness, hatred, and even indifference impacts us. Not letting go of these things is a defense reaction. We will protect ourselves, corrupting the very journey on which God is drawing us into intimacy with Himself.

Sheep are a bit resistant to drink from running water, even though it can be fresh and may be better at resisting contamination. The shepherd will guide his sheep by the streams he has made still.

How has the Lord addressed your fears in the past? Is there resistance on your part to Him revealing with what is fearful in you? Does "future casting" blind you to the waters of peace?

> "He refreshes *and* restores my soul (life)" (Psalm 23:3 AMP).

If I am cast down, my seeking Shepherd comes and puts me back on my feet. He restores my inner being.

A cast sheep could die or be vulnerable to predators. When locating a cast animal, the shepherd gets it to its feet and rubs its legs until it can walk.[1]

Restoration is a rigorous activity by the shepherd to return the sheep to health or power. In our "cast down-ness" we can lose sight of the Shepherd's healing intentions to correct us.

> "Why are you in despair, O my soul? Why have you become restless *and* disquieted within me?" (Psalm 42:11 AMP).

David speaks of the self murmuring him into despair because

of the taunts of his opposition. The challenges of life goad us into hopelessness. The critical self-talk roars in our thinking, and our world gets turned upside down.

Restoration is a process to bring us in line with who God created us to be. Reproof is our Lord educating us, adjusting us to genuine wholeness.

In college I was introduced to Dr. John Clark, a chiropractor who offered me his services free of charge. He explained his work would be with just my neck region. If the two vertebrae on which my skull sets were in line, my entire vertebral column would adjust, thus affecting my whole body.

What did I have to lose? After x-rays of my neck, he had me lie on my side and marked the focus area of adjustment. Then he stood over me, and with both hands clasped together, pressed down with the heel of his hand.

I didn't feel a thing. No snap, crackle, or pop! He warned, "In two or three days you will feel as if you have the flu. Call and come in immediately."

Right, I thought.

In three days I woke thinking I was going to die. I had fever, chills, and nausea. I called Dr. Clark and asked a friend to take me in. The doctor used the same procedure, and all the symptoms faded.

He explained I was so far out of adjustment, the therapy had a strong side effect. With his continued patient treatment, I eventually felt much better.

The Holy Spirit can use stress as a way of correcting us, restoring us to integrated thinking, a process in which our thought processes are brought into balance. This procedure creates an openness and freedom in responding to life.

What stressful situations has He used to correct you? How did you react to His restoration activity? What did you discover about God and yourself?

As He restores, then …

"He leads me in the paths of righteousness for His name's sake" (Psalm 23:3 AMP).

He continually guides me into rounds of fresh pastures by the paths He knows, overseeing my life into higher places by His right-making ways, revealing the wonder of His heart.

No other class of livestock requires more attention than sheep, and the owner's reputation depends upon his care. Pasture management not only reflects on the shepherd, but creates an environment for the sheep to be what they were created for.[2]

For God to transform those patterns of thinking that harm us, He continually calls us into a journey, a path which changes us more and more into Christ's likeness.

What are the right-making activity of the Lord in your life? What attitudes, values or relationships is He making right in you? How is He bringing that about?

"Even though I walk through the [sunless] valley of the shadow of death, I fear no evil, for You are with me" (Psalm 23:4 AMP).

He guides through deep ravines of menacing predators and torrential storms. I have come to fear no evil because I have come to know the Shepherd in a deeply personal way in this place of shadows.

These gorges are also waterways in which the guided sheep find refreshment. In addition, the richest feed and best forage can be found there. Predators and the challenge of summer storms can also be expected.[3]

Note the I-Thou relationship, there is a change in pronoun from He to You (the Shepherd). As He leads them to the higher meadows through the ravines, the sheep draw closer to the shepherd.

A shadow is cast on a surface, such as a wall, by an object illuminated by light.

What evil is challenging you? What are your reactions? What light has the Shepherd thrown on it?

> "Your rod [to protect] and Your staff [to guide], they comfort and console me" (Psalm 23:4 AMP).

Your rod of authority gives me victory, and your staff guides me in the conquest.

The staff and rod were made from the same sapling; thus the rod of victory and the staff guidance are a part of each other. That is, His victory over evil is in His transforming presence.

Often the question comes, "Why didn't God protect me or my loved ones more? Why didn't He intervene in such a horrific act?"

It is only as we allow ourselves to be drawn to Him that we eventually come to know His heart concerning this matter. This truth does not come easily; our pain affects our thoughts concerning our most profound relationship—the one with God. However, as we journey authentically through the pain, eventually allowing the Shepherd access there, He will be the Truth we need to know: victory in His reshaping presence.

> Jesus answered, "I am the way and the truth and the life. No one comes to the Father except through me." (John 14:6)

As you walk with Me, you will discover the Reality of who I Am, your Life, and come to know the Father.

Recall those places you came to know His presence as your Victory. In what way did He reshape the experience? Is there an unfinished issue hindering the Shepherd from drawing you to Himself?

Since 1982, I've had the unique privilege of working with clients who deal with sexual trauma, horrific family violence, and the brutality of war, natural disasters, and indescribable grief. In the safe environment of a nonjudgmental listener, they gradually opened their wounds. They invited me to explore with them the unspeakable torment affecting their life.

Their wholeness was realized, not only resolving the effects of the pain but through revealed insights about God's heart and intentions there.

Each client comes to an understanding of their own about God's presence in those horrendous experiences. His intervention was God Himself.

What I came know through these gallant victors was this: I had the choice as to not only how I dealt with my dad's alcoholic violence perpetrated on my mother and me but how open I was to God's presence there. It was only then I found purpose in those painful places. Moreover, I offer to you the gifts of those wounds, this resource you hold in your hand.

"You prepare a table before me in the presence of my enemies" (Psalm 23:5 AMP).

You are arranging a table of communion, healing, and provision in the very sight of those exposed as hostile and opposed to my presence there.

As the shepherd has led his flock up into the mountain ranges, he sets in order a table mat for the sheep to feed in the company of the life-threatening predators. The mat is made from the skin of a sheep or lamb that has been slain.

Paul defines the ground of our enemies: "Do you think anyone is going to be able to drive a wedge between us and Christ's love for us? There is no way! Not trouble, not hard times, not hatred, not hunger, not homelessness, not bullying threats, not backstabbing, not even the worst sins listed in Scripture" (Romans 8:35 MSG).

The table prepared in the presence of the enemy is the table of communion. It reaches beyond the Lord's Supper, or the Eucharist, or the Table of Communion we celebrate with fellow members at church.

The life sacrificed, the lambskin, calls us to meet with Him in the face of our adversary as identified by Paul. It is there we can come to embrace the wonder of His body given and His blood shed.

Think on how much it cost the Father to buy our redemption and that of others, no matter how diverse. Our willingness to recognize the gift of divergent people is revealed in our life of communion and openness to the Holy Spirit.

It is in this intimacy we can enable others to grow if they choose to. To love without condoning or condemning.

During a Networks of Our World plenary session, the Rev. John David shared the story of his own self-discovery regarding hatred. Rev. David was instrumental in designing eighteen Committees of Reconciliation commissioned to bring a peaceful end to apartheid, the rigid governmental separation of the nonwhite population.

Because of his leadership opposing and protesting apartheid, he became the target of a white Dutch commander. Cutting telephone wires, slashing tires, and intimidating church members were parts of the violence perpetrated by this commander upon Pastor David and his family and followers.

Begrudgingly, he joined a Green Weekend in the bush sponsored by Africa Enterprise, where each participant told the story of their life and the issues that brought them to their personal and political position.

The facilitator asked each contributor to write down the person who caused them pain and hatred. Joseph quickly wrote the commander's name. He was then instructed to list all reasons for the pain and hate caused by this named individual. He vigorously began to write out every event, experience, and encounter. He was delighted; now someone would listen and get it.

Then the facilitator asked them to scratch out that name and put their own. Peter obliged.

Then came the question, "Are there any of those things listed you are not capable of doing?"

After long reflection he realized the very things he hated about this commander he found in himself.[4]

The speck in the eye of another often comes from the plank in our own eye.

What we criticize in others sows those seeds in us. Learning to grow and live in communion is eating His flesh and drinking His blood. His embodied obedience and suffering in us creates His life through us to embrace those we see as different from us.

In order for us to know God's commitment to all people, we must come to know the depth in which the Father worked in His Son; for it is in that same depth He must work in us. This is communion.

Is there an irritating person in your life? Is it possible the Holy Spirit wants to reveal something in you with regard to this person?

What is it about certain people that makes you uncomfortable in their presence?

"You have anointed *and* refreshed my head with oil
(Psalm 23:5 AMP).

You have rubbed and anointed my head with oil.

During rutting, mating, he applies a heavy grease to the heads
of the monarchs as they collide in combat over the ewes. Also, the
shepherd rubs the heavy oil up the sheep's noses to protect them from
botflies. They will burrow up the nose and lay eggs, which hatch and
destroy the brain. During fly time, if the shepherd does not anoint
the sheep, they become frantic, butting their heads against rocks or
refusing to eat.[5]

As a watering hose can get kinked and alter the flow of water
from the spigot to the nozzle, daily experiences and relationships
become "kinked" by processes in our minds we are not conscious of.
"Nose flies" of negative thoughts are so deeply burrowed in the brain
pathways that they affect our communion with Him and our trust
in others. He desires to anoint our thinking, unkinking our brain,
to know the reality of His presence and authenticity in relationships.

Here the Shepherd is healing our thinking when it comes
to relating to one another. We act out "kinked-up" thinking in
relationship to others: butting heads—conflicts, anger, competition,
one-upmanship—has to do with how our brain processes those
relationships

The resonating circuitry in our brain is the pathway connecting
us one to another. We are to join with the Holy Spirit in knowing
this reality, for He is the Spirit of Truth.

"There is a world of difference between knowing something
to be true in your head and experiencing the reality in your life,"
explains Henry Blackaby.[6]

Is God showing you patterns of "kinked-up" thinking? If so,

how is He going about revealing this truth to you? How are you reacting? What do you need to do?

In the face of David's adversary, the Shepherd provided a slain lambskin table of communion. Smoothing his mind with the oil of protection and healing, he experiences an enlarged capacity an abundant life.

"My cup overflows" (Psalm 23:5 AMP).

The cup is our capacity for an overflowing life. As we surrender to the Shepherd drawing us to himself as our protection through the valley, He shows us He is present in the face of hostility. It is here we are empowered to meaningfully embrace and encounter life in all of its beauty and pain, contradictions and joy. It is here the display of His rightness and his right-making intentions is encountered.

Think about a small stream with narrow banks on each side. Its capacity to carry water is limited. However, if you widen the banks, it can move a greater volume of the life-giving water.

David affirms, "Hear me when I call, O God of my righteousness: thou hast enlarged* me when I was in distress; have mercy upon me, and hear my prayer" (Psalm 4:1 KJV).

Whatever straits David was encountering, he contends his right-making God exploited (made the most) of that very adversary to establish and to enlarge his ability to deal with life's challenges.

Have there been settings in which God used adversity to enable you to become more understanding and forbearing? Tolerant of others? Less judgmental? What were they?

What resources has the Shepherd given enabling you to so?

"Surely goodness and mercy *and* unfailing love shall follow me all the days of my life" (Psalm 23:6 AMP).

Because of the gracious ownership of my shepherd, beauty and loving-kindness will arise out of my life to bless others.

Well-managed sheep can be the most beneficial livestock. Their droppings can create fertile lands. They can consume weeds, which choke out good vegetation. After several years, his flocks left behind them beautiful, productive lands.

Recount and thank the Shepherd for the benefits He has created as you follow Him.

"And I shall dwell forever [throughout all my days] in the house *and* in the presence of the LORD" (Psalm 23:6 AMP).

Because of who the Shepherd is, I will dwell in His shepherding all the length of my days.

The sheep are so cared for, they have no need or desire to be under another shepherd.

As we come to realize His daily pasturing, His sheltering, we are drawn by this journey to truly want none other than living in His presence under the Shepherd's leadership—His kingdom reign.

Steep your life in God-reality, God-initiative, and God-provisions. Don't worry about missing out. You'll find all your everyday human concerns will be met.

Give your entire attention to what God is doing right now, and don't get worked up about what may or may not happen tomorrow. God will help you deal with whatever hard things come up when the time comes. (Matthew 6:33–34 MSG)

Our priorities naturally arise out of what we value.

What's become more important to you as you live under the reign of Christ and His right-making ways?

Living like Jesus with Each Other

The Beatitudes are not a series of disconnected thoughts. They are movements into a deeper relationship and a manifestation of life with others. Much like a spiral staircase—with four steps leading inward and the others leading outward—these truths build on one another.

Jesus is describing in this message of the Beatitudes the reality of authentic relationships under His reign. Although the kingdom is top-down under His authority, it is bottom-up in the realization of relationships. He is unfolding the characteristics of those submitting to Him as King and relating to each other in mutual loving obedience.

This sermon is about living right-side-up in an upside-down system, the world.

> "When Jesus saw his ministry drawing huge crowds, he climbed a hillside. Those who were apprenticed to him, the committed, climbed with him. Arriving at a quiet place, he sat down and taught his climbing companions" (Matthew 5:1–2 MSG).

As we began our journey with "the Jesus guys," let's climb together with Him and listen as He speaks to us about what it means to live out the reality of His reign over us and with each other in this dislocated system called the world. Think what it would be like to be there, to be one of His apprentices. Think of the crowd and our impact on their lives.

What is the "crowd" in which you are called to live out Jesus's reign? Which ones are the most challenging? What is that about? Are there companions enabling you to climb with Him? What is it about them that makes it so?

In prayer with men from our church I sensed the Lord saying, "You give the guys all kinds of room to fail, and you love and respect them. What keeps you from respecting Me when I don't meet your expectations?"

Shattered, weeping, I openly confessed my sin and knew forgiveness, both His and theirs.

As we climbed with Jesus together through our sharing, I discovered a self-absorbed sense birthed out of the gilded pretense that all was great with my birth family. I could not let others know how embarrassed I felt living in the system of alcoholism my entire family was affected by. We were all alcoholics.

My life as a kid was a fabrication, a secret I had shouldered for years. Now I realized it had been meddling with my mind regarding the group and their view of me.

Listen as Jesus continues:

"You're blessed when you're at the end of your rope.
With less of you there is more of God and his rule"
(Matthew 5:3 MSG).

God's desire is to meet us at the end of our self-centered ways. He reigns there. We, with tightened grip, hang on to those things we believe are our identity.

Where have you experienced being at the end of your rope? Reflect; what did you come to know about God's compassionate control? Are you now in a situation and find yourself at the end of your rope? How are you reacting?

"You're blessed when you feel you've lost what is most dear to you. Only then can you be embraced by the One dearest to you" (Matt. 5:4 MSG).

When we come to an end of agendas and self-centeredness, we can experience loss and grief, even if the adjustment results in something positive or growth in mind or spirit.

Grief

Loss is suffered by everyone. How we process loss indicates how well we are. We are involved in loss other than death. In order to grow, we must let go of certain attachments, expectations, dreams, and illusions. In order to flourish, we will have to relinquish misconceptions about God.

When I first came to Calvary Baptist Church, Hayward, many were affirming the healing of an adored woman of the congregation. Along with the former pastor, they had claimed verses of healing and held special prayer meetings for her deliverance. Yet she died.

It was my task to help them understand "believing" in itself, even with scriptures, can become an end in itself. Believing about believing, no matter how fervent, can mislead us.

I led them to reflect on their view of God and what they had to change, now that He had said no. Did some have certain attitudes they needed to confess? Hurt feelings they needed to own?

Looking back, I wanted them to see the difference between expectations and expectancy.

Expectations focus on the believing, or belief in the believing. If we believe hard enough, God will come through and can leave us defeated and confused if the scripture we are standing on is not answered.

Expectancy, like hope, is the confidence God is working for our best, even though we may not at that time comprehend His activity.

List those dreams and expectations you have given up. What were your feelings? Can you identify when you're grieving these losses? What did you come to know about the Lord and yourself?

Appendix F, Stages of Loss, will aid you in understanding the effects of loss

> "You're blessed when you're content with just who
> you are—no more, no less. That's the moment you
> find yourselves proud owners of everything that
> can't be bought" (Matthew 5:5 MSG).

As we embrace loss into growth, we can be empowered to be more at ease and satisfied with who we are becoming in God's sculpting process. There is palatable gratification in being who we are.

As we allow loss to do its work and burn out the dross of our own self-centered desires, we can discover the God-intended place for us, contented, comfortable in our own skin where we are. It's been there all the time.

Insight

> "Adversity is like a strong wind. I don't mean just
> that it holds us back from places we might otherwise
> go. It also tears away from us all but the things that
> cannot be torn, so that afterward we see ourselves

as we really are, and not merely as we might like to be" (Arthur Golden).[7]

Eugene Peterson in The Message describes this state of being as our "God-created self."

It is imperative to understand, as believers in Jesus Christ, that the essence of who we are—this core—occurs only by the new birth. This is the crux of the Christian life. The Holy Spirit is committed to freeing us to live as the soul of who God created us to be—nothing less than resurrection living.

Rehearse and write down some of those formation moments in this journey of growth. Are you able to see these as your God-created self moving into greater freedom? Where is He at work right now?

> "You're blessed when you've worked up a good appetite for God. He's food and drink in the best meal you'll ever eat" (Matthew 5:6 MSG).

Indeed, what is happening through this realization is a yearning to spend time with Him. So, I'm going to pause and attend to Him.

Jesus contends that when we are open to be who we are, the Spirit has free will to create a hunger to know God. We want to truly know His heart.

God also yearns to spend time with us. He paid such a costly price to do so. He calls us to know His presence in the valley as in the mountains.

This is intimacy—"in-to-see-me." As I am open to allow His Spirit to see me, I have a hunger to know God's heart.

With the groups I'm involved with, and especially my wife, Sue, only to the degree I am willing to let them see into me will I know intimacy with God (and they will let me in to see who they really are).

How do you react to the foregoing statement? Is this true of your relationships? Are there safe places you can let yourself be authentic?

> "You're blessed when you care. At the moment
> of being 'care-full,' you find yourselves cared for"
> (Matthew 5:7 MSG).

As God's Spirit brings us through our deepening walk, He is in the process of shifting us into a place of genuine care for others, an expression outward.

"Love is the will to extend one's self for nurturing one's own or another's spiritual growth ... love is as love does. Love is an act of the will ... an intention and an action. Will also implies choice. We do not have to love. We choose to love" (M. Scott Peck).[8]

Rather than caretaking or inappropriate enabling, which have self-centered motivations, we find ourselves caregiving, empowering, and freeing others to grow if they so choose.

What relationships are stimulating, growing, and yet challenging for you? What makes them so? How have you grown spiritually in them?

In what relationships do you spend time and energy which are not appreciated? In which do you ignore offensive behavior or begrudge an obligation you have to take on? Perhaps you are caretaking instead of caregiving (see Appendix G: Care-Taking Instead of Caregiving).

> "You're blessed when you get your inside world—
> your mind and heart—put right. Then you can see
> God in the outside world" (Matthew 5:8 MSG).

In authentic care for others, our mind and heart become adjusted to encountering Him in our daily lives.

When we join God in truly caring for others, we will find Him all over.

Story

A third of the TCF congregation were developmentally disabled mentally or physically, which turned off many who visited the church. However, those of us who knew them found the wonder of love, humility, and tenacity.

Ricky, a young teenager in a wheelchair due to spina bifida, started attending the church. His family noted a change. He became more-sure of himself. He felt useful and needed by the members. He decided to surrender his life to Christ and be baptized, which he was, in our home swimming pool. It was a decision that changed his life.

He took joy in sharing his belief in Christ with friends.

He died at age sixteen. His family reports cards and letters, mostly from teenagers, saying how he had touched their lives with prayer and a listening ear. Many stopped by the house to share how he taught them to pray for themselves and others.

> "You're blessed when you can show people how to cooperate instead of compete or fight. That's when you discover who you really are, and your place in God's family" (Matthew 5:9 MSG).

This is not a placating position, as we work for people to really connect, to honestly care for each other because of what we've gone through.

"Christ brought us together through his death on the cross. The Cross got us to embrace, and that was the end of the hostility" (Ephesians 2:16 MSG).

This act of reconciliation can cost us our right to be right.

I was blessed to be the on-site prayer coordinator for Reconciliation Networks of Our World (RNOW). Plenary sessions brought stories from all over the world of God's reconciling work in some of the most painful situations.

The impact of the stories of these witnesses on conference participants included personal repentance and restoration in their relationships upon returning home.

During RNOW Coventry, England, in November 1997, after listening to personal reconciliation encounters, I had to return home and ask forgiveness of the member of a former church who had caused me and my family deep pain.

I explained I was aware I had failed him and his expectations as his pastor, and asked for his forgiveness. He responded it was not necessary to do.

Those personal accounts of reconciliation and healing left me with no choice but to ask for forgiveness, whatever the response.

Have you encountered someone in your life who is committed to the process of reconciliation? To what extent did their openness or vulnerability play a role in healing of a personal discord?

Are you willing to offer yourself as a source of healing and resolution in conflicts you are aware of? Would the personal price be too costly?

"You're blessed when your commitment to God provokes persecution. The persecution drives you even deeper into God's kingdom" (Matthew 5:10 MSG).

You're fortunate having been hunted down because of God's approval and right-making-ness, for yours is the kingdom of heaven (author's interpretation).

What is your reaction to this comment by Jesus? What are your fears, questions, and hesitations? What has been the most difficult issue as you have honestly followed Christ into being a peace-wager?

This may sound like a strange comment from Jesus. However, as we proceed outward, seeing God in everyday places, encouraging others to reconnect and reconcile, some will react out of fear and self-protection. They will be uncomfortable with the challenge, resist, and leave us abandoned and lonely. This reality of rejection brings us to move more deeply under the reign of Christ.

> "Not only that—count yourselves blessed every time people put you down or throw you out or speak lies about you to discredit me. What it means is that the truth is too close for comfort and they are uncomfortable. You can be glad when that happens—give a cheer, even!—for though they don't like it, *I* do! And all heaven applauds. And know that you are in good company. My prophets and witnesses have always gotten into this kind of trouble" (Matthew 5:11–12 MSG).

How do they impact you? Encourage you? Discourage you? Is there anyone you know who's gone through this? Have you?

How do you react when your thoughtful intentions are

misinterpreted? Your supportive words misconstrued? Your words misread?

Someone has quipped, "Every place the apostle Paul went, he caused an uproar or revival. Every place I go, we have tea."

> Let me tell you why you are here. You're here to be salt-seasoning that brings out the God-flavors of this earth. If you lose your saltiness, how will people taste godliness? You've lost your usefulness and will end up in the garbage.
>
> Here's another way to put it: You're here to be light, bringing out the God-colors in the world. God is not a secret to be kept. We're going public with this, as public as a city on a hill. If I make you light-bearers, you don't think I'm going to hide you under a bucket, do you? I'm putting you on a light stand. Now that I've put you there on a hilltop, on a light stand—shine! Keep open house; be generous with your lives. By opening up to others, you'll prompt people to open up with God, this generous Father in heaven. (Matthew 5:13–16 MSG)

As a result of faithfulness through the Beatitude walk, we can become salt and light to others in our life. In this journey we are fashioned with the identity of His intention.

In your life are there people who have brought out God-flavors or colors? What is it about them which made them like that? Have you let them know the blessing they were?

Now let's move to another encounter with Jesus—on the lake.

The Surprise of Darkness

"Immediately Jesus made his disciples get into the boat and go on ahead of him to Bethsaida, while he dismissed the crowd. After leaving them, he went up on a mountainside to pray. Later that night, the boat was in the middle of the lake, and he was alone on land. He saw the disciples straining at the oars, because the wind was against them" (Mark 6:45–48).

Feeding the five thousand, the mass of people along with the disciples got caught in the frenzy of making Jesus into something to which He refused. Here and in Matthew, He had to force the disciples into the boat. He left them and the crowd.

There will be times we will sense Christ has left us. As here, with His followers, after a moving spiritual experience, His absence can be confusing to us.

Can you recall such an experience? What was its impact? What did you realize? What growth?

The scripture says, "He went up on a mountainside to pray." The intimate relationship of the dependent Son on His Father called Him here.

I've come to understand my prayerlessness is a symptom of my lack of dependency and intimacy with my heavenly Father.

In the same darkness that engulfed them, Jesus saw them. God does see. The gloom can blind us to this reality.

He is relentless in His pursuit of our truly knowing Him. Coming to risk Him in the inexplicable places can reveal more of who He is to us.

"Jesus, knowing that they intended to come and make him king by force, withdrew again to a mountain by himself. When evening came, his disciples went down to the lake, where they got into a boat and set off across the lake for Capernaum. By now it was dark, and Jesus had not yet joined them" (John 6:15–17).

Darkness was on the face of the sea, and they strained against the oars and were not making headway. And Jesus had not joined them.

Sound familiar? We're in common company.

Cultures; church, family, and friends can sway our perspective of God. Our own agendas color our expectations when we are following Him. Jesus sends us into dark places, and He does not show up when needed to show us these thoughts.

Have there been dark places you obeyed Him into? Places of striving and getting nowhere, where the Lord has not joined you? Are you there now?

Insight:

Keep this in mind, He separates from us for illumination. There will eventually be light in these perplexing places. He is out to introduce Himself to us in ways we have not yet known Him.

"Someone I loved once gave me a box full of darkness. It took me years to understand that this too, was a gift" (Mary Oliver).[9]

Beyond Expectations

> Later that night, the boat was in the middle of the lake, and he was alone on land. He saw the disciples straining at the oars, because the wind was against them. Shortly before dawn he went out to them, walking on the lake. He was about to pass by them, but when they saw him walking on the lake, they thought He was a ghost. They cried out, because they all saw him and were terrified.
>
> Immediately he spoke to them and said, "Take courage! It is I. Don't be afraid." Then he climbed into the boat with them, and the wind died down. They were completely amazed, for they had not understood about the loaves; their hearts were hardened. (Mark 6:47–52)

When Christ did show up, they were terrified. Even after the miracle of the feeding displayed His capability, they failed to recognize who He was on the water: He displayed splendor far beyond their expectations. They were totally unprepared for this encounter.

Are you living out of past experiences of Christ you want Him to replicate? Is that attitude keeping you from knowing Him in unprepared ways?

In our baffling and fearful places, He is saying, "Take courage! It is I. Don't be afraid."

Immediately He focused on who it was and spoke to them to be strong of heart and to stop being timid. "Center your thinking on Me, Jesus."

Story

I walked on tiptoes on the thin ice of capricious violence. I never knew when the ice would break and I would drown. Always checking, checking to be sure I could take the next step. I grew to be oversensitive to people's reactions, fearing hurt.

It took years of sharing with trusted friends, groups, and those precious churches for God to hone the fear into being sensitive to the pain in those very same relationships. They were willing in return to be authentic with me.

Where are you able to offer your pain and fears as gifts to others? What makes it difficult to do so? What have you received in return?

"Jesus's invitation 'lay down my life for others' has always meant more to me than physical martyrdom. I've always heard these words as an invitation to make my own life struggles, my doubts, my hopes, my fears and my joys, my pains and my moments of ecstasy available to others as a source of consolation and healing."[10]

Matthew resumes the story:

> "Lord, if it's you," Peter replied, "tell me to come to you on the water."
>
> "Come," he said.
>
> Then Peter got down out of the boat, walked on the water and came toward Jesus. (Matthew 14:28–29)

"Come," He said. That's all He said. That one word was enough.

In the darkness, turmoil and fear, Jesus calls His disciples to focus on the reality of His presence: "It is I." Peter, seeking confirmation, was given one word, "Come." In that moment, with his feet on His word and the awareness of Christ, he knew the wonder of being in the presence of a startling new revelation.

Dr. Daniel Siegel affirms, "Living in the moment, also called mindfulness, is a state of active, open, intentional attention on the present moment without being swept up by judgments."[11]

Being mindful is being present, attuned to the Holy Spirit.

How do you respond to this statement?

An emotional presence, such as peace, harmony, or energy, is not always indicative of His. We can easily equate the existence of these feelings, or their absence, to a belief system. We can become dependent upon them telling us whether or not we are with God.

> Let your character [your moral essence, your inner nature] be free from the love of money [shun greed—be financially ethical], being content with what you have; for He has said, "I will never [under any circumstances] desert you [nor give you up nor leave you without support, nor will I in any degree leave you helpless], nor will I forsake *or* let you down *or* relax My hold on you [assuredly not]!" So we take comfort *and* are encouraged *and* confidently say,
>
> "THE LORD IS MY HELPER [in time of need], I WILL NOT BE AFRAID.
> WHAT WILL MAN DO TO ME?"
> (Hebrews 13:5–6 AMP)

What does it mean for you to live attentive to the "I AM" of Christ?

What have you discovered regarding being conscious of God's presence? What makes it challenging for you to be attentive to Him?

The Challenge of Risking

"But when [Peter] saw the wind, he was afraid and, beginning to sink, cried out, 'Lord, save me!'" (Matthew 14:29).

God will allow the wind of circumstance to temper the reality of our trust in Him.

I know how great this makes you feel, even though you have to put up with every kind of aggravation in the meantime. Pure gold put in the fire comes out of it *proved* pure; genuine faith put through this suffering comes out *proved* genuine. When Jesus wraps this all up, it's your faith, not your gold that God will have on display as evidence of his victory. (1 Peter 1:6–7 MSG)

Story

In Ned's Canyon, next to Yosemite National Park's entrance, I'm walking with my friend Bob, a gold miner.

He's talking and looking at and kicking rocks in our path. He stops and picks up a fist-sized rock. He says it looks promising. To me it's just an ugly rock.

He will take it to the shop, crush it, and put the pieces in a hot caldron. In time he will gently scrape the slag that surfaces due to the heat. As he continues, eventually the gold will shine in its intended beauty.

"Immediately Jesus reached out his hand and caught him. 'You of little faith,' he said, 'why did you doubt?'" (Matthew 14:31).

Faith is a part of our functioning brain. It's how we choose to exercise our belief in something or someone beyond ourselves. Like Peter and Martha, we can become "double minded," our thinking split due to circumstances.

James observes, "If any of you lacks wisdom, you should ask God, who gives generously to all without finding fault, and it will be given to you. But when you ask, you must believe and not doubt, because the one who doubts is like a wave of the sea, blown and tossed by the wind. That person should not expect to receive anything from the Lord. Such a person is double-minded and unstable in all they do" (James 1:5–8).

He is not condemning but describing our split thinking, our inconsistent "doings." As pointed out, our brain is occupied with our body, time, or environment in these given circumstances. We can choose to observe this thinking without judging or fixing, giving us distance and enabling us to respond differently.

In what conditions do you find yourself experiencing misgivings in your thinking about God's love for you? What relationships or experiences have affirmed His love for you when you've mistrusted His intentions?

"Then he climbed into the boat with them, and the wind died down. They were completely amazed, for they had not understood about the loaves; their hearts were hardened" (in a continuous callous state) (Mark 6:51–52).

The guys were at a total loss to explain or grasp who He was and what He was about; they were dense as a rock, slow on the uptake. They didn't get it with the loaves; the deepest motivation, their heart, was still insensitive.

Let's not be too quick to put them down. They were on an expedition with eternity, Christ. Their reaction can help us in our own lack of insight into who He is and what He is up to: we can change our thinking.

What has been the most consistent challenge to your trusting God? Family? Finances? The future?

Be honest with God concerning your trust issues, your doubts. Rest in Him to reveal the root in your thinking. If possible, share with a trusted friend. Give Him time, without self-judgment, to do His work.

> "When they climbed into the boat, the wind died down. Then those who were in the boat worshiped him, saying, 'Truly you are the Son of God'" (Matthew 14:32–33).

The "fleshed-out" Person of God became real to them in this sequence. He will take the time He needs to "flesh Himself out" to those of us who struggle toward Him.

Go over in your mind how He has patiently worked with you before revealing who He is to you. What elements did He employ to bring this about?

Can you risk Him doing the same here? What do you need in this place?

> Who out there fears GOD,
> actually listens to the voice of his servant?

For anyone out there who doesn't know where you're
going,
    anyone groping in the dark,
Here's what: Trust in GOD.
    Lean on your God!
But if all you're after is making trouble,
    playing with fire,
Go ahead and see where it gets you.
    Set your fires, stir people up, blow on the
    flames,
But don't expect me to just stand there and watch.
    I'll hold your feet to those flames.
(Isaiah 50:10–11 MSG)

He is impassioned about being our worth. The basic word for worship is "that which is worthy," living in reference to what carries weight in our decisions, what we bow down to.

How we spend time, finances, or energy lets us know what really carries weight with us in practical, everyday choices. Idolatry can be investing worth to something other than what we were created for.

Our idolatry can focus on relationships, success, comfort, or financial sufficiency.

His demand they eat His flesh and drink His blood was revolting to them (see John 6:48–58). His blood was to be the source of redemption. His body was to be the embodied expression in them to be like Him. Their reaction prompted Him to shove them with an expected negative query.

From that time on many of his disciples turned back
and no longer followed him.

"You do not want to leave too, do you?" Jesus asked the Twelve.

Simon Peter answered him, "Lord, to whom we shall go? You have the words of eternal life. We believe and know that you are the Holy One of God." (John 6:66–69)

The traverse from the feeding, through darkness, and the dialogue with the crowd wakened their responsive spirits to the words that He was the very sustenance of their life. For years I've ask groups and clients what keeps them steadfast in following the Lord even through the darkness of doubts, confusion, personal failure, divine silence, or negative influences of family, finances, or circumstances challenging their commitment?

"I can think of no other choice than staying the course, even when I don't know where that path may lead," a friend of mine affirmed.

Or another: "I've been there—bitter, angry, and hopeless—and found those places were a dead end. For me, faith is refusing to go there even if I don't know what is going on with God."

What is it which keeps you taking the next step? How did that come about?

In April 1521, Martin Luther was called before Holy Roman Emperor Charles V at the Diet of Worms—a formal meeting at Worms, a city south of Frankfurt. Luther thought he would have a chance to defend his ideas. Charles would only accept an ironclad recantation. What Charles got was Luther's defiant speech.

At the end of his speech he spoke the famous words, "Here I stand; I can do no other. God help me" (even though there is some question if Luther said this at that time).[12]

Faith is often when we can do no other. Have you been there? What keep you going? What came out of that place for you?

Growing Up: Abram

> The Lord had said to Abram, "Go from your country, your people and your father's household to the land I will show you.
>> I will make you into a great nation,
>>> and I will bless you;
>> I will make your name great,
>>> and you will be a blessing ...
>> and all peoples on earth
>>> will be blessed through you."
> (Genesis 12:1–3)[13]

Reflect to a time when God called you to grow spiritually—to move beyond relational expectations, plans, aspirations, or dreams to a new direction in life. Was it a gradual loosening of your grip? If so, what aspect was most challenging? Or was it perhaps a complete break? What were the reactions of those close to you?

Who or what encouraged you? Specifically, what blessings have you experienced? In what way has this experience of growing up and moving on blessed others?

Abram and Lot arrive in Canaan, eventually having to separate because "the land could not support them while they stayed together, for their possessions were so great that they were not able to stay together. And quarreling arose between Abram's herders and Lot's .... The LORD [spoke] to Abram after Lot had parted from him" (Genesis 13:6–7, 14).[14]

Abram had a difficult time moving on in faith. Although he did so, it was not until Abram was pressured by conflict.

Don't allow the last hesitancy in obedience to define your next step. The Lord sees the eventual outcome of our struggles when they are from a heart which desires to obey.

What challenges are you facing in your next step of faith? Is your last misstep or indecision affecting your next step in faith? Are there stresses pushing on you to do so?

Abandoned to Bless: Joseph

> Joseph's master took him and put him in the prison, a place where the king's prisoners were confined; so he was there in the prison. But the LORD was with Joseph and extended lovingkindness to him, and gave him favor in the sight of the warden ....
>
> Pharaoh said to Joseph, "Since [your] God has shown you all this, there is no one as discerning *and* clear-headed and wise as you are. You shall have charge over my house, and all my people shall be governed according to your word and pay respect [to you with reverence, submission, and obedience]; only in [matters of] the throne will I be greater than you [in Egypt]." (Genesis 39:20–21; 41:39–40 AMP)

Discarded by his brothers, betrayed by Potiphar's wife, tossed in prison, forgotten by the butler, Joseph was eventually empowered by Pharaoh.

God displayed Himself through Joseph in prison, to reveal Himself in the palace. Joseph was abandoned to bless.

At times, others are successful, and we're stuck in a dead-end situation. Others are recognized, and we waste away in the shadows. We ask God to meet us in these places, and there is silence.

One of the most difficult issues I faced was why God would lead me into such a painful church environment after His activity and blessing in Hayward. Over six years my family and I were exposed to harsh criticism, backbiting, and rejection. Over six years He was silent to my pleading.

But out of the womb of agony He not only birthed a remarkable church but a life of prayer in me and in the church.

This was when I came to know from experience that the succession of devastations was God's intention to be gracious to us.

> "Therefore the LORD waits [expectantly] *and* longs to be gracious to you, and therefore He waits on high to have compassion on you.
>
> For the LORD is a God of justice; blessed (happy, fortunate) are all those who long for Him [since He will never fail them]." (Isaiah 30:18 AMP)

What prolonged situation of "stuck-ness" have you known? What surfaced in you? How has God revealed Himself to you? Or is He still silent?

Perhaps you are in that trapped condition. What is it like for you to be there?

Opposed or Opportunity: Paul in Prison

> Now I want you to know, believers, that what has
> happened to me [this imprisonment that was meant
> to stop me] has actually served to advance [the
> spread of] the good news [regarding salvation] ....
> [T]he brothers have renewed confidence in the
> Lord [seeing that God can work His good in all
> circumstances] .... For to me, to live is Christ [He is
> my source of joy, my reason to live] and to die is gain
> [for I will be with Him in eternity]. (Philippians
> 1:12, 14, 21 AMP)

In prison, Paul exclaimed Christ was his life. In that reality he
impacted his guards and brothers. His life was not defined by his
circumstance.

Circumstances can either enslave us or empower us, revealing
what is our true source of life.

What conditions are defeating you? What is that about? Or what
ones are inspiring you?

Are you depending upon circumstances to do these things?

What would change if you truly responded, "to live is Christ"?

Christlike Thinking: Authentic Communicating

Do nothing out of selfish ambition or vain conceit. Rather, in humility
value others above yourselves, not looking to your own interests but
each of you to the interests of the others. In your relationships with
one another, have the same mindset as Christ Jesus:

Who, being in very nature God,
  did not consider equality with God
something to be used to his own advantage;
rather, he made himself nothing
  by taking the very nature of a servant,
  being made in human likeness.
And being found in appearance as a man,
  he humbled himself
  by becoming obedient to death—
    even death on a cross!

Therefore God exalted him to the highest place
  and gave him the name that is above every
  name,
That at the name of Jesus every knee should bow,
  in heaven and on earth and under the earth,
and every tongue acknowledge that Jesus Christ is
Lord,
  to the glory of God the Father.
(Philippians 2:3–11)

This is a significant statement regarding interpersonal relationships: valuing others above ourselves. It demands Christlike thinking.

He had to let go of His entitlement. In embracing servanthood, He was truly human. And He became obedient to the cross and is realized as Lord of Lords.

As a communication coach with couples, I lead them to understand Christlike listening requires a process of letting go of perceived entitlements or holding on to bitterness, anger, or demands; each becoming a servant by putting themselves in the other's mindset, and dying to their own defenses of explanations, excuses, and denials. In this listening process Christ's lordship is realized.

In transactions with others, we can find ourselves being defensive rather than setting aside our rights. Authentic listening requires us to set aside our explanations, defenses, and judgments and seek to listen beyond the words to the heart.

Reflect on the situations which may stimulate defensive reactions from you. What do you observe? Can you work behind them to the thinking that drives your reactions? If so, what is it?

Or how do you react to those who are defensive toward you?

With whom or what do you need to change? What would happen if you did?

Captured: Paul

> Not that I have already obtained all this, or have already arrived at my goal, but I press on to take hold of that for which Christ Jesus took hold of me. Brothers and sisters, I do not consider myself yet to have taken hold of it. But one thing I do: Forgetting what is behind and straining toward what is ahead, I press on toward the goal to win the prize for which God has called me heavenward in Christ Jesus. (Philippians 3:12–14)

After trashing his advantages being a Jew—reckoning them as "dog dung" (MSG)—Paul nurtures passions to know and live out the power of the resurrected Christ (Philippians 3:1–11).

He has been captured, and he is driven to seize that for which he has been apprehended: Christlikeness every day, living the resurrection. Nothing less.

What advantages in the past have you counted on which now you see as constraining your desire to be Christlike? What brought about the change?

Harassed by Go: Jacob

But Jacob stayed behind by himself, and a man wrestled with him until daybreak. When the man saw that he couldn't get the best of Jacob as they wrestled, he deliberately threw Jacob's hip out of joint.

The man said, "Let me go; it's daybreak."

Jacob said, "I'm not letting you go 'til you bless me."

The man said, "What's your name?"

He answered, "Jacob."

The man said, "But no longer. Your name is no longer Jacob. From now on it's Israel (God-Wrestler); you've wrestled with God and you've come through."

Jacob asked, "And what's your name?"

The man said, "Why do you want to know my name?" And then, right then and there, he blessed him.

Jacob named the place Peniel (God's Face) because, he said, "I saw God face-to-face and lived to tell the story!" (Genesis 32:24–30 MSG)

God will "risk" being misunderstood so we can come to truly know His heart and our real identity.

Think back to what you now realize was God-initiated experience in which you came to have more clarity about who you are. What was significant about the encounter?

When you realize, like Jacob, you're trying to work out things on your own, even with the best intentions, and it all falls apart, how do you react?

"God is too good to be unkind and He is too wise to be mistaken. And when we cannot trace His hand, we must trust His heart."[15]

Authenticity and Pain: Jeremiah

> Those who were my enemies without cause
> hunted me like a bird.
> They tried to end my life in a pit
> and threw stones at me;
> the waters closed over my head,
> and I thought I was about to perish.
>
> I called on your name, LORD,
> from the depths of the pit.
> You heard my plea: "Do not close your ears
> to my cry for relief."
> You came near when I called you,
> and you said, "Do not fear."
> (Lamentations 3:52–57)

Lamentations is a topography of unequaled suffering and pain in Zion and the prophet Jeremiah. He was held by a passion for his people to embrace the truth in the pain. The cumulative decades of national idolatry and rebellion against God's heart for His beloved came cascading down as a tsunami of His judgment without His intervention. The silence of God's voice in this book bears witness to this fact.

This book bears witness: There is a place for genuine lamenting. Where pain cannot speak, truth cannot be known.

Life-Insight: Tony

Faithful to God and his church, Tony came to me with a dilemma. Ten years prior to our meeting he'd had an amazing God encounter to surrender his all to Christ. However, instead of a deeper sense of relationship with his Lord, there was emptiness, a palpable distance in their relationship.

He endured through the years with this perplexing matter haunting him. Why would God call him to such a submission of his life and then seemingly abandon him? He was fraught with doubts. How could he now come to God with all these misgivings about His heart?

I encouraged him to talk about his reservations, his doubts. As we listed them, he was challenged to bring them to God—to be honest and open regarding where he was spiritually and "dump" those issues on God's lap.

He fiercely resisted: "How can I do that, pushing Him further away?"

"He already knows your heart issues. What He wants is for you to face them in His presence. Just as with your kids, you want them to be open, even about those things you know they are dealing with. The lack of openness is what's causing the problem."

I also explained to him he was not to declare these issues as sins at this time. He was too confused and shame-bound to know what to confess. He would eventually come to see what needed to be acknowledged as sin.

With tears and his list, Tony started to honestly bring his doubts and fears to God in prayer. As he persisted, slowly, over a time, Tony began to let go of the shame and receive God's grace.

"I've discovered He loves me in the midst of the doubts and fears. I kept resisting His grace to accept me as I was."

Pain has a language of its own. When we get real with others and God, it becomes a sacred vocabulary; we acquire a wisdom about ourselves, life, and God, inspiring those in their own suffering.

Does it sound too self-pitying or seem like an excuse to blame God? Have you encountered truth birthed in spoken pain? Your reaction?

What is your reaction when someone retches in pain over an absent God (as with Tony and his pain)? How do you react? Can you be comfortable without answers, just be present?

Giving Yourself Away: Jesus

"For this reason the Father loves Me, because I lay down My [own] life so that I may take it back. No one takes it away from Me, but I lay it down voluntarily. I am authorized *and* have power to lay it down *and* to give it up, and I am authorized *and* have power to take it back. This command I have received from My Father." (John 10:17–18 AMP)

Until we know this, we will not know where to legitimately lay down our life and will continue to define our worth by others' response rather than God's.

> "Each of you should use whatever gift you have received to serve others, as faithful stewards of God's grace in its various forms ... so that in all things God may be praised through Jesus Christ. To him be the glory and the power for ever and ever. Amen" (1 Peter 4:10–11).

Sue has contended I tell silly jokes and terrible parables. So here is a terrible parable.

A friend begs you to rescue an abused mutt from the pound. You consent. The puppy is delivered. You feed and take loving care of your dog. You study about abused animals. You take it to training classes. Things are going well. You feel good!

One day you go to feed it, and it mauls you. You persist, and it keeps happening. If you just try hard enough, just keep hoping, things will change.

But the animal charges you every time you attempt to care for or feed him.

How could that dog so such a thing after all you've done?

The failure exposes a flaw in your thinking: no matter how hard you try, you cannot make the mutt into Lassie. The warm glow dies into ashes.

Embracing the truth, you grieve and start feeding the dog on the other side of the fence.

Many of my female clients present as being intelligent, hardworking, and loving. Yet they are married to men who abuse them verbally, emotionally, or physically. Each is convinced if she tries harder, loves more, or does more, the man in her life will change.

Facing the inevitable, they seek to understand the drives which open them to the pain. They began by joining with God in this work of discovering their value to Him. These women understand God calls them to be faithful stewards in surrender to Him first of all. And out of that, as a gift to others. They start to grow by developing appropriate expectations of themselves and their husbands.

One of the most difficult things each of us has to face is this: we must realize that our relationships or situations we attempt to change, to make them into something they will never be, will compel us to face not only our powerlessness but also to realize, no matter how hard we try, we cannot expect them to bless us or give us meaning or significance.

Without being aware of it, we think if we can work hard enough with someone or move a situation into a place of change, we will be accepted or affirmed. The reality that we cannot shape something according to our own desire or design is a very difficult truth we have to acknowledge. Often we hang on to a mutt-type situation that keeps us from following Christ in obedience.

Second, in this process we can become open to feeding the mutt from behind a fence—in other words, to be disengaged. This means believing we can be in a relationship and not allow it to determine our worth, which we can eventually find in Jesus Christ.

A steward is one who looks after or administers another's resources. We have been purchased by the blood of God's Son; we no longer belong to ourselves. As we become heart-aware of the costly transaction of the cross, we will be less given to cheap bidders of life.

Our worth is reflected in the boundaries we keep or the commitments we make to others.

What relationships or systems have you allowed to take your life from you? What has been your reaction? What would be the most challenging if you began to take your life back? How would you go about this challenge?

Humility: Paul

What is your understanding of humility?

> Living then, as every one of you does, in pure grace, it's important that you not misinterpret yourselves as people who are bringing this goodness to God. No, God brings it all to you. The only accurate way to understand ourselves is by what God is and by what he does for us, not by what we are and what we do for him ….
>
> [L]let's just go ahead and be what we were made to be, without enviously or pride fully comparing ourselves with each other, or trying to be something we aren't. (Romans 12:3, 5 MSG)

Humility is an appreciation living contented with my limitations. It is a true knowing of myself as I am. Shame, the belief we are defective, perverts humility.

As water seeks low ground, the presence and glory of God seek lowliness.

Recent studies show humility is connected with many forms of prosocial behavior. While some misunderstand humility as low self-esteem or self-denigration, a proper conception of this virtue has both self-regarding and other-regarding components. Humble people keep their accomplishments, gifts, and talents in a proper perspective. They have self-knowledge and know their limitations as individuals and as human beings. But humble people are also oriented toward others; they value the welfare of other people and have the ability to "forget themselves" as well, when appropriate.

Humble people have better social relationships, avoid deception in their social interactions, and tend to be forgiving, grateful, and cooperative. A recent set of studies also shows humility is a consistent predictor of generosity.[16]

Writing to the church in Ephesus, Paul was continually overwhelmed by God's grace, he was amazed he had been delivered and could be used in such a way to touch so many for the sake of the gospel (see Ephesians 3:1–2, 7–8.)

What have you to come to know about yourself, your limitations, and your "not-ness"? In what way has this insight about yourself caused you to stand in wonder regarding His grace rather than shame regarding your shortcomings?

What influences has God used to bring you to this place? Has this self-knowledge changed your relationship to God and others? If so, in what way? Can you accept your mistakes as being normal?

Strangleholds: Goliath

A giant nearly ten feet tall stepped out from the Philistine line into the open, Goliath from Gath. He had a bronze helmet on his head and was dressed in armor—126 pounds of it! He wore bronze shin guards and carried a bronze sword. His spear was like a fence rail—the spear tip alone weighed over fifteen pounds."

> Goliath stood there and called out to the
> Israelite troops …. When Saul and his troops heard
> the Philistine's challenge, they were terrified and
> lost all hope. (1 Samuel 17:4–8, 11 MSG)

Life-Insight: Morgan

She's in crisis, a former client, and calling me. Her married son, Mack, is accused of impregnating an old flame. His marriage is in jeopardy, there are financial liability issues, and the family name at risk.

"I've been walking around like a zombie. I don't know what to do." She carries on with a litany of impending doom scenarios.

Breaking in on the barrage I ask her to step back take a breath and reflect for a moment on those thoughts without judging them.

"I can't help my son. He's old enough. I should know better."

Breaking in, "You're judging yourself. Be open, stay objective, and observe your thoughts."

"I can't help him. I'm helpless."

She wanted to fix things but had no answers.

"So what does that mean to you?"

"I'm failing my son. I'm a disappointment."

Then the light dawned. "Oh, there's my old thinking," she replied. Without realizing it, she had been brought down by an old negative perception, negative cognition, and "I'm a disappointment."

She began to understand why "turning it over to God" was not working. It was not a lack of faith but the way her past patterns were reacting to the present situation.

On the phone, she released the mess to God, confessed her fear of being a disappointment, got back her mojo, and hung up. Later she called to follow up. She had informed Mack this was his issue, and until he had a viable plan and was acting on it, he was not to bring up the situation.

Mack in turn decided to take a paternity test and learned he was not a match. He went on to confront the woman on his own.

In her phone conversation, Morgan was prompted to reflect and allow her emotions to be what they were without being drawn into them. It was her thinking, driven by feelings of being incapable, that had led her into crisis.

What was the signal Morgan was being affected by old thinking patterns? How was she reacting? What was the core negative belief?

A colossus can reign in our thinking without our knowing it. Negative, destructive beliefs influence how we perceive God, ourselves, and others. It is an unconscious narrative whispering in our thoughts in stressful settings. It's like a thermostat turning on in a room when its gets too cold or too hot; we are, for the most part, unaware of its input.

In what circumstances are you most aware of Goliath's taunts? How do they affect you? Do you get stuck there?

Is there a situation in which God's love for you is hard for you to buy into and receive? What are you aware of? What within you is making it so?

"Living unloved is like clipping a bird's wings and removing its ability to fly. Not something I want for you."

Mack did not feel particularly loved at that time.

"Mack, pain has a way of clipping your wings and keeping you from being able to fly." She waited a moment, allowing her words to settle. "And if left unresolved for a very long time, you can almost forget you were created to fly in the first place."[17]

Story

In Crystal Butte, Colorado, winter snow swathed the mountains, welcoming a retreat for young people from a Texas Baptist and Pentecostal congregation. Invited to lead the evening Bible study, I explained to the leader, my nephew, my concern regarding what the Lord had laid on my heart to share: the story of the pain I and my family had in pastoring a church; thoughts about my leadership and preaching; and what I was discovering about God, His love, and His presence there. He assured me the timing was spot-on for such a message.

Monday evening, forty or so mustered around a fireplace with their Bibles as I read scriptures regarding believers' call to shoulder the cross of submission in their daily life.

I recounted the hurt I felt I had caused the family and myself, even though I knew God had called us to this church. I was honest regarding the despair, the anger, the bitterness, and the doubt I was going through, the insights about God's heart, embracing Christ's pain over His bride, this church and all those hurting by it and in it.

Tuesday morning my nephew let me know how upset the Baptist kids were regarding Monday night's study. (By contrast, the Pentecostal youth really bought into my thoughts.) I had violated the viewpoints of these conventional Baptist kids, and they were offended.

I was crushed. Exposing my truest feelings had wounded the very people I ached over to experience this Christ I had come to know in such precious moments of intense adversity.

I spent the morning scourging my ineptness, my very existence. Echoes of past voices haunted me. Words I cannot repeat here sledgehammered me steadily into a consuming despair.

Grabbing my Bible like a drowning man in a storm grasping for a life preserver, I tore it open. Somewhere in the recesses of my mind I recalled the story of Goliath in 1 Samuel 17.

He was gigantic, dwarfing a normal soldier, consistently vilifying Saul's commandeered army. The warriors defined God by Goliath.

Then up shows David, an abandoned sheep boy, neglected by a dad, slandered by his older brother, unfit for warrior gear, victor over bear and lion, in his sling a stone, in his heart God. Prepared by those experiences in the sheepfold, David defined Goliath by his God.

A cascade of truth, then love, then joy washed over me. I was then able to confront my real giant: I hurt people. The rest of the week I could somehow speak loving truth to those young people.

Honestly, I still get taunted by Goliath every once in a while. However, I am learning to invite Jesus to meet me there in those hecklings and to praise Him audaciously. No giving in to my accusing brain, just praising Him. I'm coming to experience His love there.

Discontentment: Naomi

> In the days when the judges ruled, there was a famine in the land. So a man from Bethlehem in Judah, together with his wife and two sons, went to live for a while in the country of Moab …. Now Elimelek, Naomi's husband, died, and she was left with her two sons. They married Moabite women, one named Orpah and the other Ruth. After they had lived there about ten years, both [sons} also died, and Naomi was left without her two sons and her husband. (Ruth 1:1, 3–5)

The grass is always greener on the other side of the fence. Yeah, and it's usually over a septic tank.

Whenever Bethlehem, the "House of Bread," has no bread, the scarcity, either in relationship, resources, or promise, drives us to look for the "fields of Moab." Greener grass. Living in the "if only" of the discontent, we travel to the very place culminating in "without-ness."

Perhaps the "famine" we experience is instigated by the decisions of others or our own choices. Nonetheless, we chafe at the lack.

Reflect: If there is personal famine, what is it? Who or what triggered it? Are there expectations, dreams, or promises that have died? Where does this leave you? How are you dealing with the dearth in relationship, resource, promise, or potential?

Paul to the Philippians:

> I'm glad in God, far happier than you would ever guess—happy that you're again showing such strong concern for me. Not that you ever quit praying and thinking about me. You just had no chance to show it. Actually, I don't have a sense of needing anything personally. I've learned by now to be quite content whatever my circumstances. I'm just as happy with little as with much, with much as with little. I've found the recipe for being happy whether full or hungry, hands full or hands empty. Whatever I have, wherever I am, I can make it through anything in the One who makes me who I am. I don't mean that your help didn't mean a lot to me—it did. It was a beautiful thing that you came alongside me in my troubles. (Philippians 4:10–14 MSG)

In the place there should be bread but there is none, can you affirm with Paul, "whatever I have, wherever I am, I can make it through anything in the One who makes me who I am'?

Reality Check: Jesus

> Now when He was in Jerusalem at the Passover feast, many believed in His name [identifying themselves with Him] after seeing His signs (attesting miracles) which He was doing. But Jesus, for His part, did not entrust Himself to them, because He knew all *people* [and understood the superficiality and fickleness of human nature], and He did not need anyone to testify concerning man [and human nature], for He Himself knew what was in man [in their hearts—in the very core of their being]. (John 2:23–25 AMP)

Story: Divine Perspective in Uncertain Times

> So if you're serious about living this new resurrection life with Christ, *act* like it. Pursue the things over which Christ presides. Don't shuffle along, eyes to the ground, absorbed with the things right in front of you. Look up, and be alert to what is going on around Christ—that's where the action is. See things from *his* perspective. (Colossians 3:1–2 MSG)

Unpredictability can be among the most disturbing issues we experience during this virus crises. Because of the loss of stability, we can feel depressed and choose to slow down and think about what is significant in life.

We're going to encounter this painful place: however, how we react is our responsibility. There are ways we can work with the Holy Spirit to "see things from his perspective."

First, know that the sense of feeling flat, the loss of energy, is a form of grief. Write a letter about the loss, or talk to a friend. Give yourself permission to grieve. Call people who may need encouragement. Read about or watch funny movies. Pace yourself. Get exercise, but don't overdo it.

Above all else, look for those things, places, and people you can be thankful for.

> Rejoice always *and* delight in your faith; be unceasing *and* persistent in prayer; in every situation [no matter what the circumstances] be thankful *and* continually give thanks *to God*; for this is the will of God for you in Christ Jesus. (1 Thessalonians 5:16–18 AMP)

Who is it you can call to either share your burdens or encourage them? What are those things, resources, or people you are thankful for? What else can you do to work with the Holy Spirit to see things from God's viewpoint?

Messing Up in a Mess: James

> If any of you lacks wisdom [to guide him through a decision or circumstance], he is to ask of [our benevolent] God, who gives to everyone generously and without rebuke *or* blame, and it will be given to him. But he must ask [for wisdom] in faith,

without doubting [God's willingness to help], for the one who doubts is like a billowing surge of the sea that is blown about and tossed by the wind. For such a person ought not to think *or* expect that he will receive anything [at all] from the Lord, *being* a double-minded man, unstable *and* restless in all his ways [in everything he thinks, feels, or decides]. (James1:5–8 AMP)

At the very beginning of this survival manual for the dispersed Jewish believers, James contends wisdom and wholeness can issue from the consequence of running into different kinds of difficulties. The indication here is the problems can be our own creation. He even asserts this encounter can be a source of joy when we keep that truth clearly in mind.

He maintains as we work through these difficulties, we eventually create the capacity for spiritual growth, an integration of our thinking and behaving, every part brought into a wholeness (see James 1:4).

Daniel Siegel expounds: "Well-being emerges when we create connections in our lives—when we learn to use mindsight (reflective skills) to help the brain achieve and maintain integration, a process by which separate elements are linked into a working whole."[18]

Integration is the scriptures' portrait of holiness—a whole life; Christlike thinking and behaving. As we submit to His refining in troubles, everyday life becomes more open to God's possibilities.

James encourages us to seek God's insight or wisdom to put all this together. However, he explains we can become split-minded when tossed by winds of circumstance and informs us this split-mind thinking can keep us from receiving what God has for us there.

Think back to a hardship you experienced. Who or what helped you work through it to a healthy thinking reality? Even joy?

Is there a situation you are struggling with presently? What makes it so?

Punished or Educated: Hebrews

> My dear child, don't shrug off God's discipline,
>   but don't be crushed by it either.
> It's the child he loves that he disciplines;
>   the child he embraces, he also corrects.
>
> God is educating you; that's why you must never drop out. He's treating you as dear children. This trouble you're in isn't punishment; its *training*, the normal experience of children …. But God is doing what *is* best for us, training us to live God's holy best. At the time, discipline isn't much fun. It always feels like it's going against the grain. Later, of course, it pays off handsomely, for it's the well-trained who find themselves mature in their relationship with God. (Hebrews 12:4–7, 10–11 MSG)

One of the effects of this disconnect caused by Adam is the self-protective part of our brain is primed to believe bad things are going to happen to us, to keep us out of harm's way. The brain's electrical activity is more stimulated by unpleasant than by pleasant news. Political smear campaigns outpoll positive ones.

We get hammered by the effects of living, because life is hard. If we have a negative view of God, we are biased in regard to the ways He moves to speak with us in these difficult moments. Instead of being open to His loving correction, we are convinced He is punishing us.

I'll ask clients, "What if God is not punishing you in this tough situation?"

The usual comeback is, "Then what do I do with that if He is not punishing me?"

They begin to explore why they perceive God as bad.

Looking back, what were the experiences during which you thought you were being punished, but now you see them as God enlightening you about His love?

Are there settings which make it hard for you to believe God is treating you as His dear child? If so, why?

The Synchronized Life: Habakkuk

Though the fig tree does not bud
    and there are no grapes on the vines,
though the olive crop fails
    and the fields produce no food,
though there are no sheep in the pen
    and no cattle in the stalls,
yet I will rejoice in the Lord,
    I will be joyful in God my Savior.

The Sovereign Lord is my strength;
    he makes my feet like the feet of a deer,
    he enables me to tread on the heights.
(Habakkuk 3:17–19)

Habakkuk petitioned and complained to God regarding the invading Babylonian armies and their abusive pillaging of Judah, the chosen people of God. This doesn't make sense.

In the desolation of fig trees, grape vineyards, olive crops, barren fields, sheep pens, and cattle stalls he sets his mind and heart to rejoicing. In the honesty of sharing his pain, Habakkuk came to live in the larger reality of God's dominion, the refining of His people for a greater design—God's revealing of Himself in flesh, Jesus the Christ.

The portrait is of a small, fragile female dear scampering the heights far above her male counterpart. The reason: her gait is perfectly synchronized as she negotiates rocky, uneven places— because God has made her for just such agile sure-footedness. She is a display of balance and integration.

Integration is a process by which separate elements are linked together into a working whole. It allows us to be flexible and free in life. If not, the lack of balance in our thinking can lead to rigidity or confusion and an inability to make healthy connections with God and others.[19]

All through 2020 and Sue's death in January 2021, God had coordinated the right doctors in the right places, emergency room personnel, family gatherings and support, and hospice care in such synchronicity it was jaw-dropping to everyone involved. Again He spoke to my heart.

It is imperative I be open to His work in synchronizing my walk with Him. I am to stay present to the moment, resist past failures and future fixing, and be aware of what is happening around Him.

I am no longer a pastor or counselor, no longer involved in mission activity or now, most significantly, a husband. What am I to do and be? As I have grieved all these losses, the Lord has revealed that, just as He orchestrated these events with Sue, He was calling me to be in sync with Him daily.

His presence is to be my purpose, my "high places."

I am a classic type A personality: competitive, ambitious, and organized, and I hate to waste time. So I have spent much of my time multitasking. That drive can take me past being attentive to the Holy Spirit.

I am to deliberately take on one task at a time, slow down, and pace myself.

I will still have to integrate all the losses into my life. I am to grieve authentically, incorporating these experiences in my journey. I am to take care of myself, getting the rest I need, journaling, walking, joining a grief group, taking to friends, and eating right.

Are there incidents in which you find yourself being inflexible or in turmoil? Is it possible God's aim is to refine your thinking to embrace greater purpose, His presence?

Chained to the Chariot: Paul

> But thanks be to God, who always leads us in triumph in Christ, and through us spreads *and* makes evident everywhere the sweet fragrance of the knowledge of Him. For we are the *sweet* fragrance of Christ [which ascends] to God, [discernible both] among those who are being saved and among those who are perishing; to the *latter* one an aroma from death to death [a fatal, offensive odor], but to the other an aroma from life to life [a vital fragrance, living and fresh]. And who is adequate *and* sufficiently

qualified for these things. (2 Corinthians 2:14–16 AMP)

The triumph was a ceremony awarded to a victorious Roman general. Those he conquered were chained to his victory chariot and displayed before the citizens as they were dragged through the streets of Rome.

Paul refers to an intentional surrender to Christ. He displays those of us who are chained to His chariot as life to those who are being made whole, toward more wholeness; and death to those on their way to self-destruction, toward more self-destruction.

Yielded to His victory, we are led through thoroughfares that can humble us and yet bring the knowledge of Christ through us to those we live among.

In Paul's letter to the Colossians he makes use of the same word: "Having disarmed the powers and authorities, he made a public spectacle of them, *triumphing* over them by the cross" (Colossians 2:15).

The word *powers* as used in the New Testament is fluid. It can mean the demonic but also any earthly system which has lost its God-purposed intentions. The implications here are weighty. Whether demons, governments, businesses, churches, or marriages, intentionally yielding our control or our wrist to His victory can have deep impact in these places. Christ can then display His character as Victor.

In what places are you raising your fist rather than surrendering your control? What intentional steps is He inviting you to take toward surrender?

The yielded wrist has more do to with our attitude toward His conquest of us as we continue to be faithful to Him, whatever the outcome of that surrender.

Six

RESURRECTION: THE STATE OF ONE AWAKENED FROM DEATH

I have been crucified with Christ and I no longer live, but Christ lives in me.
—Galatians 2:20

Christ and His Cross

(November 2018) I'm in a Catholic retreat center as I write this to you. The room is simple in setting. On the wall is a crucifix. I've spent some time looking at it, reflecting on how much He went through to purchase us. I'm overwhelmed with gratitude to Him for this expression of His care.

As you read, be present to what is happening as if you are a disciple of Christ or one of the women who followed Him. As you see Him crucified, what are your thoughts? Your feelings? What would it be like to be one of the soldiers who mocked Him or divided His clothes? Or to be Simon? You are not there as an intellectual exercise but a participant.

Break up the passage, reflect as the person or people in the passage.

Then the governor's soldiers took Jesus into the Praetorian and gathered the whole company of soldiers around him. They stripped him and put a scarlet robe on him, and then twisted together a crown of thorns and set it on his head. They put a staff in his right hand. Then they knelt in front of him and mocked him. "Hail, king of the Jews!" they said. They spit on him, and took the staff and struck him on the head again and again. After they had mocked him, they took off the robe and put his own clothes on him. Then they led him away to crucify him.

As they were going out, they met a man from Cyrene, named Simon, and they forced him to carry the cross. They came to a place called Golgotha (which means "the place of the skull"). There they offered Jesus wine to drink, mixed with gall; but after tasting it, he refused to drink it. When they had crucified him, they divided up his clothes by casting lots. And sitting down, they kept watch over him there. Above his head they placed the written charge against him: THIS IS JESUS, THE KING OF THE JEWS.

Two rebels were crucified with him, one on his right and one on his left. Those who passed by hurled insults at him, shaking their heads and saying, "You who are going to destroy the temple and build it in three days, save yourself! Come down from the cross, if you are the Son of God!" In the same way the chief priests, the teachers of the law and the elders mocked him. "He saved others," they said, "but he can't save himself! He's the king of Israel! Let him come down now from the cross, and we will believe in him. He trusts in God. Let God rescue him now if he wants him, for he said, 'I am the Son of God.'" In the same way the rebels who were crucified with him also heaped insults on him.

From noon until three in the afternoon darkness came over all the land. About three in the afternoon Jesus cried out in a loud voice, *"Eli, Eli, lema sabachthani?"* (Which means "My God, my God, why have you forsaken me?").

When some of those standing there heard this, they said, "He's calling Elijah."

Immediately one of them ran and got a sponge. He filled it with wine vinegar, put it on a staff, and offered it to Jesus to drink. The rest said, "Now leave him alone. Let's see if Elijah comes to save him."

And when Jesus had cried out again in a loud voice, he gave up his spirit. (Matthew 27:27–50)

What are you aware of? How does this story speak to you? What is most meaningful in the story? Take time to rehearse that part.

This may be the most challenging section in this resource. Personally, it is most difficult to write and perhaps convey. I put these words to the page, praying what I am attempting to express can be the most liberating truth for you.

The Self-Absorbed Life

"Then Jesus said to his disciples, 'Whoever wants
to be my disciple must deny themselves and take up
their cross and follow me. For whoever wants to save
their life will lose it, but whoever loses their life for
me will find it'" (Matthew 16:24–25).

The single most challenging stop is what George Barna identified as
"Stop 7, which is brokenness." The researcher indicated in order to
move closer to completion of the journey, a person must be broken
of three things: sin, self, and society. He noted America's culture
serves as a strong barrier to people being willing to completely
abandon themselves and the world in favor of listening to, obeying,
and enjoying God.

An individual cannot transform himself, nor can
a church transform a person. That work can only
be done by God, through the empowerment and
direction of the Holy Spirit. But God is eager to
partner with those who will cooperate with Him.
Understanding what God seeks to do in our lives
is a critical step toward not becoming seduced
and sidetracked by mere religious activity. The
richness of the journey is found in the experience of
progressing through the challenges of the process in
the company of God.[1]

Our core identity is freed from adaptations, forgeries, and
dominations birthed out of the systems we create in order to survive
life.

It is imperative for us as believers in Jesus Christ to understand the essence of who we are—this core—is restored only by the new birth. This is the crux of the Christian life. The Holy Spirit is committed to freeing us into the soul of who God created us to be, nothing less than resurrection living—Christlikeness.

The Real Issue

"God does not give us more than we can bear!" Words spat at me in anger. Clients have heard this declaration from pulpits and well-meaning friends regarding their agony suffered without answers. They are not salved with expected relief from those applying such assurances. The death of a child, unrelenting pain, spiritual darkness without end, the loss of a job, crises in the family—the list goes on.

The cross we are called to is not the litany just recited. All of us suffer tragic events in life. The issue is how we eventually come to relate to these experiences. Living out a Christlike life, resurrection living, spiritual formation—this only comes through daily relinquishing the adaptations, manipulations, and control we selfishly demand of God and others. God calls us into His activity of bringing about death to our self-centeredness and creating authentic life out of our Spirit-birthed core self.

When the Holy Spirit diagnoses a sinful mindset in our lives, His intention is surgery. He will urge us to the operating table, under the bright light of self-examination, and require our hand to be in His as He begins. The deeper the finding, the deeper the work. We will lunge from the table of procedure and find Him drawing back time and time again. He knows our heart, how desperately we hunger for intimacy with God and His presence. We finally come to know: the deeper the work, the greater the healing. The greater the healing, the more abundant the life.

That table is the cross we are called to carry.

> We who have this spiritual treasure are like common clay pots, in order to show that the supreme power belongs to God, not to us. We are often troubled, but not crushed; sometimes in doubt, but never in despair; there are many enemies, but we are never without a friend; and though badly hurt at times, we are not destroyed. At all times we carry in our mortal bodies the death of Jesus, so that his life also may be seen in our bodies. Throughout our lives we are always in danger of death for Jesus' sake, in order that his life may be seen in this mortal body of ours. This means that death is at work in us, but life is at work in you. (2 Corinthians 4:7–12 GNT)

Paul was in prison for including the disregarded gentiles in the Gospel. He maintained it was his turn to follow Christ in his own suffering: "Now I rejoice in my sufferings for your sake, and in my flesh I am filling up what is lacking in Christ's afflictions for the sake of his body, that is, the church" (Colossians 1:24 ESV).

John Piper discloses,

> What is lacking in the afflictions of Christ is not that they are deficient in worth, as though they could not sufficiently cover the sins of all who believe. What is lacking is that the infinite value of Christ's afflictions is not known and trusted in the world. These afflictions and what they mean are

still hidden to most peoples. And God's intention is that the mystery be revealed to all the nations. So the afflictions of Christ are "lacking" in the sense that they are not seen and known and loved among the nations.[2]

Though Piper is here referring to missionaries, the same truth holds for you and me. God calls us to be on mission with Him so others will come to know His crucified love.

When we embrace life events, not as victims, martyrs, or ascetics, we eventually come to see we are displaying the unfinished suffering of Christ. Sharing in His suffering is a result of faithful obedience to Christ.

> One day when large groups of people were walking along with him, Jesus turned and told them, "Anyone who comes to me but refuses to let go of father, mother, spouse, children, brothers, sisters—yes, even one's own self!—can't be my disciple. Anyone who won't shoulder his own cross and follow behind me can't be my disciple .... Simply put, if you're not willing to take what is dearest to you, whether plans or people, and kiss it good-bye, you can't be my disciple." (Luke 14:25–27, 33 MSG)

Ruthless words from the sweet and gentle Jesus. However, the problem is not just in themselves and our relationships, it's the deep-seated part of us that creates and sustains an idolatry concerning those relationships. We will fashion conditions around a narcissism which uses others in the place of our Creator – either to control or placate.

"For my part, I am going to boast about nothing but the Cross of our Master, Jesus Christ. Because of that Cross, I have been [and continue to be]* crucified in relation to the world, set free from the stifling atmosphere of pleasing others and fitting into the little patterns that they dictate" (Galatians 6:14 MSG).[3]

How do you respond to cross bearing as being on mission with God so others will know His crucified love through you?

Can you identify those patterns of pleasing others and fitting into the little patterns they dictate? What situations is God using to grow you to be like Christ? How do you react?

This issue goes to the heart of trusting Christ – how do we faithfully respond to Him shackled with the constant agony of ailments of soul and body?

He has said to me, "My grace is sufficient for you [My lovingkindness and My mercy are more than enough—always available—regardless of the situation]; for [My] power is being perfected [and is completed and shows itself most effectively] in [your] weakness." Therefore, I will all the more gladly boast in my weaknesses, so that the power of Christ [may completely enfold me and] may dwell in me. So I am well pleased with weaknesses, with insults, with distresses, with persecutions, and with difficulties, for the sake of Christ; for when I am weak [in human strength], then I am strong [truly able, truly powerful, truly drawing from God's strength]. (2 Corinthians 12:9–10 AMP)

"Weakness," here refers to an ailment which deprives someone of accomplishing that which is intended; it focuses on the disability which goes with a handicap.

What is sorely needed is a genuine expression of Christ's presence in the midst of such agony of soul and body. Not martyrdom, but an honest, open life, faith-abandoned to the intentions of Christlikeness in the suffering.

When have you been able to identify with Paul's affirmation of Christ's sufficiency in his weakness? If so, in what way?

We're mindful of Job. Divine permission having granted devastation, loss, and agony, he drags himself through a blitzkrieg of condemning judgment. Complaining, he is finally confronted with holy sovereignty. He has had to face the real issue of his life—repentance.

Job answered GOD:

> "I'm convinced: You can do anything and everything.
>   Nothing and no one can upset your plans.
> You asked, 'who is this muddying the water,
>   ignorantly confusing the issue, second-guessing
>   my purposes?'
> I admit it. I was the one. I babbled on about things
> far beyond me,
>   made small talk about wonders way over my
>   head.
> You told me, 'Listen, and let me do the talking.
>   Let me ask the questions. *You* give the answers.'
> I admit I once lived by rumors of you;

now I have it all firsthand—from my own eyes
and ears!
I'm sorry—forgive me. I'll never do that again, I
promise!
I'll never again live on crusts of hearsay, crumbs
of rumor."
(Job 42:1–6 MSG)

I have had the privilege of working with committed Christians in Israel, Palestine, South Africa, India, South Korea, and England. I've asked for their viewpoint regarding the church in America. In candid conversations, they shared their opinions with me. I've penned their responses in a poem entitled "The Wrong Side of the Cross" (I've used "the Brits," for they convey the position of the rest).

The Wrong Side of the Cross

'Em Yanks live on the wrong side of the Cross,
　　They got the cart before the horse,
　　Want the power without the cost,
So our Brit brothers say.
There ain't the glory without the death,
　　ain't no growth without the test,
　　ain't no victory without the stress,
So our Brit brothers say.
The only way to power is to be weak.
The only way to the heights is to be meek.
The only way to be close is to seek,
So our Brit brothers say.

Transformation

"I assure you *and* most solemnly say to you, when you were younger you dressed yourself and walked wherever you wished; but when you grow old, you will stretch out your hands *and* arms, and someone else will dress you, and carry you where you do not wish to go." Now He said this to indicate the kind of death by which Peter would glorify God. And after saying this, He said to him, "Follow Me [walk the same path of life that I have walked]!" (John 21:18–19 AMP)

Confronting Peter with the reality of his commitment—affection rather than allegiance, Jesus predicted a radical transformation: Peter would eventually die on a cross because of his commitment to his Lord.

He said to him, "Follow Me [walk the same path of life that I have walked]!" (John 21:19 AMP).

Simply put: with the walk comes the change.

In scripture, *walking* has to do with a day-by-day lived-out faithfulness to Christ, even in the middle of trying circumstances or ambivalent emotions.

Remember, ultimately the way the Holy Spirit deals with our narcissism is by crucifying our self-centeredness—the adaptations, control, and manipulations. Through this process we experience the power of the resurrected Christ—Christ-likeness. Called to be real.

In the Velveteen Rabbit, the rabbit asked the wise Skin Horse about becoming real.

"Does it hurt?" asked the Rabbit.

"Sometimes," said the Skin Horse, for he was always truthful. "When you are Real you don't mind being hurt."[4]

In what way is God calling you to be authentic?

Deciding

I gave up all that inferior stuff so I could know Christ personally, experience his resurrection power, be a partner in his suffering, and go all the way with him to death itself. If there was any way to get in on the resurrection from the dead, I wanted to do it. (Philippians 3:10–11 MSG)

As we hunger for intimacy with Christ, we can become confused by the inexplicable personal pain involved in satiating that desire.

It has been said the blood deals with what we have done—sinned against our Creator. The cross deals with what we think—entrenched in surviving, the lies we believe about ourselves, others, and God.

As you have traveled with Christ, has there been a shift in your understanding of the price He paid for you?

Drawn

Then Jesus made it clear to his disciples that it was now necessary for him to go to Jerusalem, submit to an ordeal of suffering at the hands of the religious leaders, be killed, and then on the third day be raised up alive. Peter took him in hand, protesting, "Impossible, Master! That can never be!" (Matthew 16:21–22 MSG)

The very place of His death is the place of His resurrection. Jerusalem, the flash point of rigid religious powers under the domination of a system demanding subjugation—Rome. So we will find ourselves called to die in the place of unredeemed powers and relationships to reveal His life in us.

Work and growth continue, and we are discovering life in Christ and with each other. Although we still have issues, we are now able to talk about and resolve them.

Of the relationships you find yourself in, which has affected your freedom in Christ? Are there patterns God uses to reveal how self-protective you are? Perhaps defensive? Are you becoming aware of the unconscious lies creating walls between you, God, and those relationships?

Commune

When it was time, he sat down, all the apostles with him, and said, "You've no idea how much I have looked forward to eating this Passover meal with you ...."

Taking bread, he blessed it, broke it, and gave it to them, saying, "This is my body, given for you. Eat it in my memory."

He did the same with the cup after supper, saying, "This cup is the new covenant written in

my blood, blood poured out for you." (Luke 22:14–
20 MSG)

His closest followers had designs for themselves, which He absolutely demolished. In this place of execution of self-perpetuated desires or dreams, He desires for us to know His presence in the bread and juice—the broken bread of His embodiment through our brokenness and the juice of His loving commitment to make His life a reality in and through us to others.

What does it mean for Him to be bread and juice?

Surrendered

Again he prayed, "My Father, if there is no other way than this, drinking this cup to the dregs, I'm ready. Do it your way."

When he came back, he again found them sound asleep. They simply couldn't keep their eyes open. This time he let them sleep on, and went back a third time to pray, going over the same ground one last time. (Matthew 26:43–44 MSG)

Jesus encountered one cumulative experience of Gethsemane for all of us. However, there is in us an ongoing struggle of surrender in the many arenas of daily living—multiple Gethsemanes.

As Jesus refused to concede to the expectations and demands of His disciples, our personal Gethsemanes of abandoning ourselves to God's will can conflict with loved ones' designs for us. Often the struggle is so personal we can't explain what's going on; sometimes we don't even know.

Are you willing not to know so you can know Him?

"No"

God did answer His prayer. He said no.

The Father said to His Son, "No, Son, You will drink the cup."

> "The man from whom the demons had gone out begged to go with him, but Jesus sent him away, saying, 'Return home and tell how much God has done for you.' So the man went away and told all over town how much Jesus had done for him" (Luke 8:38–39).

He said no to the one He had freed from demons.

> Paul and his companions traveled throughout the region of Phrygia and Galatia, having been kept by the Holy Spirit from preaching the word in the province of Asia. When they came to the border of Mysia, they tried to enter Bithynia, but the Spirit of Jesus would not allow them to. So they passed by Mysia and went down to Troas. During the night Paul had a vision of a man of Macedonia standing and begging him, "Come over to Macedonia and help us." After Paul had seen the vision, we got ready at once to leave for Macedonia, concluding that God had called us to preach the gospel to them. (Acts 16:6–10)

He said no to Paul.

God's "No" to His Son was for a greater purpose beyond the

dreams, plans, and imaginations of those who loved and followed Him: the redemption of humankind.

Our Gethsemanes are a call to submit God's "no" for the greater design—moving us toward Christlike living in the power of His resurrection as a witness to others.

In my life I've often struggled with this mystery of His "no."

Gethsemane can be the gut-wrenching demand to give up what is most precious to us, our will. "Yet not as I will, but as you will" (Matthew 26:39).

What is your most significant experience of God's "No"? What was your initial response? Have you come to embrace His "No"? If so, how did that come about? What has come out of that "no"?

When filming the 2011 film *Contagion*, Marion Cotillard admits she did not understand everything the director, Steven Soderbergh, was doing in the film. "I found it interesting to allow myself to be lost, because I had this amazing guide …. You abandon yourself for a story and a director will make it work."[5]

Have you been willing to abandon, to be lost to the story of Christ?

Betrayed

Five times John recounts Jesus being handed over and His reaction (John 18–19).

> "Now Judas, who betrayed him [who handed him over], knew the place" (John 18:2).

> "'I am he,' Jesus said. (And Judas the traitor was standing there with them)" (John 18:5).

Isaiah 53 identifies Jesus Christ with us the transgressors. Those who betray us can cast us in the worst light by their own agendas. "He [willingly] poured out His life to death, and was counted among the transgressors; ... And interceded [with the Father] for the transgressors" (Isaiah 53:12 AMP).

God desires to fashion this experience of betrayal into a place of intercession for others who have been betrayed. And we will eventually pray for the very ones who betrayed us and thus be so identified with our Lord others who know this pain will be drawn into the same fellowship.

God is most moved by this place of betrayal as the "sweet smelling sacrifice." "During the days of Jesus' life on earth, he offered up prayers and petitions with fervent cries and tears to the one who could save him from death, and he was heard because of his reverent submission. Son though he was, he learned obedience from what he suffered" (Hebrews 5:7–8).

If we cling to the pain and bitterness of the incident, we not only resist the healing offered there; we can refuse God the pleasure of reaching those perpetrating the pain and those who have encountered the same betrayal. This is the essence of intercession.

What support, if any, do you have working through your hurt of treachery? Or you attempting to be a "Lone Ranger" in this experience? How is that working for you?

How do you react to the thought of praying for the perpetrators? Or offering your pain in the place of those who have been betrayed?

Accused

"If he were not a criminal," they replied, "we would not have handed him over to you" (John 18:30).

After standing before the religious powers, Jesus was dragged before the political powers and deceitfully indicted by lies.

> You're familiar with the old written law, "Love your friend," and its unwritten companion, "Hate your enemy." I'm challenging that. I'm telling you to love your enemies. Let them bring out the best in you, not the worst. When someone gives you a hard time, respond with the energies of prayer, for then you are working out of your true selves, your God-created selves ....
>
> In a word, what I'm saying is, grow up. You're kingdom subjects. Now live like it. Live out your God-created identity. Live generously and graciously toward others, the way God lives toward you. (Matthew 5:43–44, 48 MSG)

I was accused of stealing $250 by a deacon of a church I pastored. I attempted to be more of a friend with him by having him go with me to different ministry opportunities. To my face he was pleasant and supportive; however, after I resigned, I discovered he had been working behind my back to get me out of the church.

At the first Reconciliation Network of Our World conference, I led the morning devotions. One of the topics was "Living in Unfixed Places" by letting go of our agendas through cross-bearing obedience.

In the closing message by Michael Cassidy, South African Christian leader and founder of Africa Enterprise, known for his initiatives at ecumenism and reconciliation, he referred to living in unfixed places. I knew immediately I was to pray for the deacon, but more so, go to him and ask for his forgiveness for failing him as his pastor.

As soon as I returned home, I went to his home.

I explained I was there to ask for his forgiveness because I had disappointed him as his pastor. He said it wasn't necessary. I had not failed him. I took the time to mention several incidents in which I had let him and others down by not meeting their expectations. He thanked me and again said he thought it was not needed.

Have you experienced accusations? How did you respond? Have been able to pray for your accusers to be blessed? If not, what is keeping you from doing so?

Dominion

"Am I a Jew?" Pilate replied. "Your own people and chief priests handed you over to me. What is it you have done?"

Jesus said, "My kingdom is not of this world. If it were, my servants would fight to prevent my arrest [being handed over] by the Jewish leaders. But now my kingdom is from another place." (John 18:35–36)

Jesus had all the muscle available to prevent the arrest which led to His death. He refused on the grounds His rule operated from another region, the kingdom of another place.

When we finally come to a confidence in His authority, His reign over us in the situation, circumstances lose their power over us.

What is your "heart reaction," your felt reaction to the above statement? Are you fighting for your rights to be heard? Understood? Known? Justified? Whose kingdom—yours or His—does your response to cruel power reveal you are operating from?

Power

> "Jesus answered, 'You would have no power over me
> if it were not given to you from above. Therefore the
> one who handed me over to you is guilty of a greater
> sin'" (John 19:11).

Jesus identifies the real source of Rome's power: God himself, using Judas to accomplish His divine intentions. As we come by faith to see the hand of God behind evil's intent, we can be open to God's loving move toward us for intimacy.

In scripture, God owns the responsibility for evil being present in this world system. He also claims accountability for evil's success.

Could it be God has a divine intention with the evil you are encountering? Are you imputing fault to the wrong person or system? Has it helped? Do you have tunnel vision to such an extent you cannot see God?

Crucified

> "Finally Pilate handed him over to them to be
> crucified. So the soldiers took charge of Jesus.
> Carrying his own cross, he went out to the place
> of the Skull (which in Aramaic is called Golgotha).
> There they crucified him" (John 19:16–18)

This is the essence of the cross: Jesus's surrender to the hands of the soldier to die, casting Himself upon the will of God. The cross and purpose of God are always beyond our own thinking. It is difficult to comprehend. Cross-bearing is not physical illness or problem relationships; cross-bearing is a voluntary embracing of God's will and larger intentions in these places.

Are you in a situation you have no control over? No matter what you do, it won't change? Where does that sense of powerlessness leave you?

> "Two robbers were crucified with him, one on his
> right and the other on his left" (Matthew 27:38).

Bearing His cross, Jesus was not only accused of being a criminal but was crucified with them. He was staked down among the most vile and yet as undiminished purity. He offers Himself to us even when we are at our worst.

Can you think about Him dying for the most despicable? If for them, why not for you?

Forgiveness

> "Jesus said, 'Father, forgive them, for they do not
> know what they are doing'" (Luke 23:34).

Let's begin with some understanding of forgiveness.

Forgiveness is a letting go of, a permitting to depart. But what do we let go of? What do we send away?

"It is not condoning, justifying, or excusing a wrongdoing. It is not getting justice or revenge. It is not going back into an abusive relationship. Reconciling is reestablishing a relationship of trust that has been damaged. It takes time and authenticity from both sides.

There are two expressions of forgiveness. They are not necessarily mutual: not in concert with each other.

Decision forgiveness is that in which we decide not to hold the wrong against the person, resolving how we will react. It has to do with our "behavioral intentions." In this process we may have to establish boundaries in order to be safe but not to seek reprisal or revenge.

As we treat the offender in a forgiving light, we will still carry feelings of bitterness, anger, or hurt. This leads us to the second type of forgiveness which may be associated with the first: *emotional forgiveness.*

Letting go of the negative emotions will be a process. We can make a decision by faith to forgive.[6]

Life Insight: Anna

Anna is a bright fiftyish woman working through sexual abuse at the hands of a grandfather, brother, and verbally sadistic mother. Promiscuous as a teen, she was later married to a jealous, physically cruel husband.

She is getting emotionally healthy, setting boundaries with her husband and family, and now dealing with the guilt of her past and the shame of submitting to the ill treatment of her husband. She is overcome with self-reproach; how could she let it happen?

Anna began to understand she was acting out the maltreatment of important people in her life as a child. I led the emerging core of the healthy self to decide to forgive the licentious self of the teen and capitulation of her unworthy self to her husband. She visited the painful litany of each act she could remember with the words "I forgive you."

The process and result took time because it eventually involved forgiving those who harmed her.

The realization was an awakening: "It's not about me!" The

liberation of that truth is having a continuous impact. She is more spontaneous, living more in the present moment. She's feeling what psychologists call self-regard; the scriptures call it humility.

React to Anna's story. Can you hear Jesus's voice whispering to forgive yourself?

Working through forgiveness, she authentically extended it to her cruel husband.

Sound crazy? I know. Pastors and counselors insisted she forgive him. When she began seeing me, her first question was "Do I have to forgive Dennis?"

"Not yet," I replied. "You are attempting to put the cart in front of the horse. We can't reconcile with another until we're more integrated or balanced in our thinking."

Through our work, she first had to process the trauma, defining how she related with others, especially her husband, Dennis. During the procedure she worked through her anger without shame, letting her husband know she needed space during this time.

Learning to communicate her feelings without attacking him, she set appropriate boundaries. She saw how wounded he was and finally confessed to me she had not only forgiven him but "liked him."

Only to the point where we can grasp being forgiven can we forgive. This is not a superficial, self-comforting act. It is coming to understand the profound cost Christ paid for our forgiveness and, from that realization, forgiving those who have wounded us.

Dip an open coffee can in a lake, and it will only hold the capacity of the can. However, if you cut out the bottom of the can, the entire lake flows through the can.

Forgiveness flows to me only to the extent I forgive others.

With the decision to forgive, the brain will continue to fire along the same neuron pathways. Once we have made the choice, our brain will continue to fire with these synaptic responses. Observe the reaction as a "brain thing," and express gratitude to the Lord for who He is—and stay with the process. Also, keep in mind synaptic stimulation affects our emotions and body sensations.

What is self-forgiveness? Basically, it is seizing God's mercy in Christ and extending it to oneself. By a faith decision we're taking ourselves off the hook of self-condemnation in our thoughts and feelings.

I found an album of photos of myself from childhood through young adulthood. As I thumbed through the pictures, I asked God and that child to forgive my rage and verbal attacks. I wept my way amid those faces and realized how resilient he was, and he did this without any adult support. I thanked God and the child for his tenacity and the gifts which came from that strength.

I became aware of a shift in my spirit. It was gradual, quiet, and, most surprisingly, evolving. I'm becoming more patient with myself and situations. I discovered the core, the rigidity of self-criticism.

Who has you on their hook because you are not willing to forgive? Are you inclined to hold resentment, anger, or bitterness against them, giving them power over you? What would it cost you if you did forgive?

Has shame bound you in self-reproach and regret? What keeps you there? Take time to confess that as sin. Then, by decision, grab hold of God's mercy, and pronounce His and your forgiveness to those incidents which have haunted you.

Remembered

"'Jesus, remember me when you come into your kingdom.' Jesus answered him, 'I tell you the truth, today you will be with me in paradise'" (Luke 23:42–43).[7]

Conquest or closeness? The thief desired kingdom success, but Christ offered Eden's relationship: "Today you will be with me."

I had to always smile—show the face, not the reality—because the reality was too terrifying, too violent, and too shameful. At that age, I had to make up stories, protect myself, display strength and not weakness, competence and not need. Be an adult, not the child.

A father too unpredictable, a mother too dependent, and a child too vulnerable—severe eye problems. "Four eyes," I was dubbed at school. Shy, ever so shy, but act friendly; show no fear. Smile; show the face, not the truth.

Ever needing a dad to be Daddy, a mom to be Mommy, while they were trying to survive each other and life and could not be present to the kid. Alcoholism was the monster robbing relationships, connections, and authentic love. Show the face, not the suffering. *Just survive* was the child's vow.

Trying to be the best I could, as good as I could, would not stop the pain, the brutality. This survival mindset constructed a life distant from God and others.

Thankfully, through God's patience and learning to "tag" those moment-by-moment feelings, I became not only able but more myself. We experience more peace by coming to identify the root cause—taking care of ourselves because we cannot believe others will.

Near

> "Near the cross of Jesus stood his mother .... When Jesus saw his mother there, and the disciple whom he loved standing nearby, he said to his mother, 'Dear woman, here is your son,' and to the disciple, "Here is your mother.' From that time on, this disciple took her into his home" (John 19:25, 27).

In the agony and violence of being crucified, Christ revealed His compassion for His mother. Her other sons (James, Joses or Joseph, Simon, and Judas) could take up the responsibility of caring for her. But they had not been "near the cross," knowing the depth of what Jesus went through. It was the "nearness" which shaped this touching moment (see Matthew 13:55–56)

As the cross calls us to faithfulness, we can discover more meaningful relationships with those who can bless and amaze us.

"We are not called by God to do extraordinary things, but to do ordinary things with extraordinary love," explains Jean Vanier.[8]

Authentic cross-bearing draws us into authentic relationships. To extend to others the possibility of spiritual growth.

As you have journeyed into a more intimate relationship with Christ, how has your closest relationship changed?

Deserted

> About three in the afternoon Jesus cried out in a loud voice, *"Eli, Eli, lema sabachthani?"* (Which means "My God, my God, why have you forsaken me?"). (Matthew 27:46)

The agony of beatings, the scourged, lacerated back, the nailed impaled hands and feet, the significant loss of blood, and the crushing darkness accumulated in the cry on the behalf of all, "Why have You forsaken Me?"

I confess this episode shatters me, the ultimate vicarious identity with us. The profound expression of love and the bearing of amassed evil, sin, and wickedness of humanity poured out on Him is overwhelming.

His was a matchless, unique experience. However, in his identity with us, and ours with Him, we can, in faithful obedience, encounter the same moments.

The call of the cross for us is to travel through the same darkness and agony in order for us to know Him in ways inexplicable. This is the heart of the Holy Spirit's work—knowing Him and living by His presence.

> More than that, I count everything as loss compared
> to the priceless privilege *and* supreme advantage of
> knowing Christ Jesus my Lord [and of growing more
> deeply and thoroughly acquainted with Him—a joy
> unequaled]. For His sake I have lost everything, and
> I consider it all garbage, so that I may gain Christ ....
> *And this, so* that I may know Him [experientially,
> becoming more thoroughly acquainted with Him,
> understanding the remarkable wonders of His Person
> more completely] and [in that same way experience]
> the power of His resurrection [which overflows and
> is active in believers], and [that I may share] the
> fellowship of His sufferings, by being *continually*
> conformed [inwardly into His likeness even] to His
> death [dying as He did]; so that I may attain to

the resurrection [that will raise me] from the dead.
(Philippians 3:8, 10–11 AMP)

Is there a present situation God is calling you to bear into the cross in order to know Christ intimately?

Do you need to take time reflecting through this passage?

Completed

"Later, knowing that everything had now been finished, and so that Scripture would be fulfilled, Jesus said, 'I am thirsty'" (John 19:28).[9]

It is thought giving Jesus vinegar would hasten His death. Also His inflamed wounds and raging fever drove Him to this last request of humankind.

As I look at the crucifix in my room, I am brought again to the absolute "done-ness" of my Lord's death. I realize when I'm ensnared by my failures or sins (which I have confessed), it is my brain snatching me down old neurological pathways. I can grab my thoughts by the neck and drag them back to the cross.

Are there relational or emotional places in which shame immerses your thoughts?

If you are still struggling with some issues, don't give up. Keep in mind "what fires, wires." That is, your brain has run those neurological pathways a long time. Again, it is not a failure of your faith.

"Jesus called out with a loud voice, 'Father, into your hands I commit my spirit.' When he had said this, he breathed his last" (Luke 23:46).

"Count the Cost" —Jesus

Having worked through to this place, how do you respond to the phase, "Just turn it over to God"? An easy out for folks "helping" us. Unless others know this journey, it's a Band-Aid doing very little good.

Until we painstakingly and honestly work through what it means to commit it to the Lord, it can become a means of denial. We become confused and frustrated.

Remember, the heart of His cross and the awful purpose behind betrayal is the granting of life to others out of His death. Thus it can be so with you and me.

> "We are not called by God to do extraordinary things, but to do ordinary things with extraordinary love" (Mother Teresa).

> "No one has greater love [nor stronger commitment] than to lay down his own life for his friends" (John 15:13 AMP).

Resurrection Life

The shattered dreams and violated trust is the broken road that became a blessing.[10]

In the pain of following Christ, where does your attention land? Has this broken road brought you back to Him? Can you eventually embrace His life being expressed to others through the hurt? Or has this journey of brokenness caused you to be defined by the anguish?

Often God seems to entice us into an inexplicable walk that

ends in the dust of death. His purpose is to introduce Himself to us there as much more than we have known of Him before: "I Am the Resurrection."

After hearing of Lazarus's death, Jesus lollygagged in Perea and then sauntered into Bethany days later.

"Lord, if you had been here ..." (John 11:21).

"I am the Resurrection and the Life ..." (John 11:25 AMP).

Mary, I Am more than your experience and expectations, more than a Healer. I Am Life.

Has the dust of death restricted your trust in God's heart for you? What keeps you from believing in His resurrection power to create something Christlike in you? Can you trust Him for more than what you have known of Him in the past?

Living out the reality of the resurrection is a journey of being transformed into the likeness of Christ. This is spiritual formation that affects our everyday living. Sometimes it is encountered as a life-altering theophany, but most often it is experienced in shifts in our thinking and relationships—or simply put, spiritual growth with insight into our pain and the pain of others. It is more than giving, going, and doing. It is Jesus bringing integration to our thinking in these areas of life.

Appendix A
NEGATIVE PERCEPTION LIST

I'm a loser.
I'm a failure.
I'm a mistake.
I'm the cause of the problem.
I'm a bother.
I'm worthless.
I'm powerless.

Search online for "Examples of Negative and Positive Cognitions.[1]

Appendix B
"ALL THE NAMES OF JESUS" LINK

https://bibleresources.org/names-of-jesus/

Appendix 6

HOW TO CREATE A
GRATITUDE JOURNAL

Jason Marsh, "Tips for Keeping a Gratitude Journal," *Greater Good Magazine*, quotes David Emmons: "Research by psychologist Sonja Lyubomirsky and others suggests journaling is more effective if you first make the conscious decision to be more grateful. Motivation to become more grateful plays a role in the efficacy of journaling,"

Go for depth over breadth. Elaborating in detail about a particular thing for which you're grateful carries more benefits than a superficial list of many things.

Get personal. Focusing on *people* to whom you are grateful has more of an impact than focusing on *things* for which you are grateful.

Try subtraction, not just addition. One effective way of stimulating gratitude is to reflect on what your life would be like *without* certain blessings, rather than just tallying up all those good things.

Savor surprises. Try to record events that were unexpected or surprising, as these tend to elicit stronger levels of gratitude.

Don't overdo it. Writing occasionally (once or twice per week) is more beneficial than daily journaling. In fact, one study by

Lyubomirsky and her colleagues found people who wrote in their gratitude journals once a week for six weeks reported boosts in happiness afterward; people who wrote three times per week didn't. "We adapt to positive events quickly, especially if we constantly focus on them," says Emmons. "It seems counterintuitive, but it is how the mind works."[2]

Appendix D

ENHANCING PERSONAL WORSHIP

Read through the suggestions completely before entering into the experience.

First, take a few moments to do the following breathing exercises. It's important to know as you breathe you are comfortable. Inhale slowly through your nose down into your diaphragm, hold the breath for a second, and then exhale slowly as if you were smoking. Pay attention to your breathing. It's as if your breath is riding the waves of an ocean or slow-moving river.

You are not attempting to relax, nor is this yoga. Slow, focused breathing activates the body's relaxation response and releases dopamine (the pleasure neurotransmitter) in the brain. Breathing slowly through your nose also releases nitric oxide, lowering anxiety, especially in socially intense situations.[3]

Be patient and try the breathing now.

Second, reflect on a beautiful place you have been to or would like to visit as you breathe. Money and time is no object. Pay attention to your surroundings—the trees, the clouds, the water—what time of day it is. Let yourself be present, not analyze, and just be. You're not in a hurry; let yourself enjoy the beauty.

Third, invite the Lord Jesus to be with you there. He just wants to spend time here with you and enjoy your presence. He paid such an ultimate price for you. You don't have to do anything, just be with Him.

This is important: what you are participating in is more than visualization. Christ is in you by the power of the Holy Spirit. This process gets you in touch with this reality.

Take time to do this when you can. It will become more effective due to the firing of neurons in your brain.

Note on Eastern meditation: research on practitioners of Eastern meditation supports the conclusion Eastern meditation unbalances the brain, contributing to a false sense of reality. The thalamus is the brain's central hub for data processing, moods, thoughts, and sensations as they are being routed to their ultimate neural destination. The thalamus also gives us a sense of what is and is not real. Subjects who have practiced Eastern meditation for more than ten years were found to have an imbalance in the function and activity of the thalamus. This would cause the practitioners to feel as if Nirvana or the state of unity with a higher power were real.[4]

Appendix E

SMALL GROUP LEADER'S GUIDE

In authentic community, there is a sense of safety and vulnerability, where people show up and can be their genuine selves. They began to respond to the real needs of their fellow group members, doing it for the reason of honoring God and each other rather than keeping to their own agenda.

1. Confidentiality is essential. We expect each person to respect and maintain the confidentiality of the group. What is said in the group will not be repeated or discussed or made a matter of prayer in any other place.
2. We are here to share our feelings and experiences and not to give advice.
3. We each share the responsibility for making the group work.
4. We accept people just as they are and avoid making judgments as to what we expect them to be.
5. We give everyone an opportunity to share.
6. We have the freedom to speak and the freedom to remain silent.
7. We give supportive attention to the person who is speaking.

8. We allow silence to do its work.

9. We are to be aware of our own feelings and to talk about what is present with us now, rather than what life was like for us in the past.

Appendix F
STAGES OF LOSS

Even though the words *stages* is used, think about the process as five piano keys. Instead of going through one stage to another, you can jump from one key to a different key and then back as if you are beginning all over. Not so. As you experience the shock of loss, even while it may have been anticipated, you can experience numbness of feelings—denial. You may move from anger to depression, back to anger, and at the same time feel numb. You are not crazy, you are "doing good grief." You don't fix grief, you do grief.

Denial and Numbness

When you're in denial about the loss, perhaps because you are numb, you try to persuade yourself or others the event hasn't happened or isn't permanent. You know the facts, of course. If your spouse has died, you might accept it happened but then believe for a time their death means nothing to you. If your parents have divorced, you might try to get them back together even after they've moved on to other relationships.

Anger and Powerlessness

Perhaps because you feel powerless, not able to fix the loss, you will feel anger. You may be angry with the person who left you, or you may feel angry with yourself. You might express the anger by shouting at people, through sarcasm, or by showing irritation at everything from significant letdowns to minor problems. This stage can also happen at any time, even after you go through a period of acceptance.

You may suppress the feeling and find it emerging as headaches, tightness in your shoulder muscles, or feelings of despair.

Bargaining and Control

At some point, you may find yourself bargaining, trying to get back what you lost. It is not uncommon to look for ways to regain control or to want to feel like you can affect the outcome of an event. In the bargaining stage of grief, you may find yourself creating a lot of "what if" and "if only" statements. It is a line of defense against the emotions of grief. It helps you postpone the sadness, confusion, or hurt.

Depression and Isolation

The depression can present with you but hard to get your hands on. You may feel sad and cry often. You might notice changes in your appetite or sleep patterns. You might have unexplained aches and pains, feelings of dullness or flatness, or loss of energy and enjoyment of usual things.

In divorce, the loss is not sharply defined as in death, it's jagged and has a process on its own. (For further understanding of divorce and grief, look up links for this subject.)

Acceptance and Rebuilding

You come to terms with the fact the "new" reality is that your partner is never coming back—or you are going to succumb to your illness and die soon—and you're okay with that. It's not a "good" thing, but it's something you can live with.

It is definitely a time of adjustment and readjustment. There are good days, there are bad days, and then there are good days again. In this stage, it does not mean you'll never have another bad day where you are uncontrollably sad. But the good days tend to outnumber the bad days. You may come out of your fog and engage with friends again, or make new relationships as time goes on. You understand your loved one can never be replaced, but you move, grow, and evolve into your new normal.[5]

Appendix G
CARE-TAKING INSTEAD
OF CAREGIVING

Someone is care-taking if they

- Find no satisfaction or happiness in life outside of doing things for the other person.
- Stay in the relationship even if they are aware the other person does hurtful things.
- Do anything to please and satisfy the other person no matter what the expense to themselves.
- Feel constantly anxious about their relationship due to their desire to always be making the other person happy.
- Use all their time and energy to give the other person everything they ask for.
- Feel guilty about thinking of themselves in the relationship and do not express any personal needs or desires.
- Ignore their own morals or conscience to do what the other person wants [6]

Be open in thinking about a relationship you have put your energy, time, and maybe finances into, giving and giving, and it has not turned out as expected. Get as specific as possible. What are your thoughts and feelings? Can you face the possibility the relationship can *never* give you what you desire? Again, don't judge; just be as present to your thoughts and feelings as possible.

Endnotes

Introduction

[1]   Joni Tada Eareckson, interview. Dr. Tim Clinton, American Association of Christian Counselors, Fairfax, Virginia (DVD, February 2011).

Chapter 1: Expedition: A Journey into Authentic Living.

[1]   Millard Baux, "Spirituality and Evangelism" (Sermon, Evangelism Conference, Flagstaff, Arizona, n.d.).

[2]   Jean Vanier, *Community and Growth*, revised edition (New York, NY, Paulist Press, 1989), 2–3.

[3]   *The Turlock Journal* (Turlock California), Letters to the Editor, June 24, 1987.

[4]   Polly McNabb, "'Wounded' Have a Place for Healing," *The California Southern Baptist Journal*, November 5, 1987. 1987-11-05-001 - California Southern Baptist Convention Digital Archive - Callimachus (oclc.org)

[5]   M. Scott Peck, *The Different Drum: Community Making and Peace* (New York, NY: Simon and Schuster Publishers, 1987), 168.

Chapter 2: Resurrection Living and Grief: Learning to Live Without

1   Rowen Williams, cited by Ruth Valerio, *Saying Yes to Life* (London, England: SPCK, 2020), 153.

Chapter 3: Wisdom, Good Sense, and Sound Judgment

1   Gary Sibcy, "Executive Function and Spiritual Growth," *Christian Counseling Today Magazine* (July 2012, Vol. 40, Issue 2), 42.

2   Laura Boyd. "How Do We Learn," *TED: Ideas worth spreading*, November, 15, 2015, https://www.youtube.com/watch?v=LNHBMFCzznE&t=4s.

3   Andrew Newberg and Mark Robert Waldman, *How God Changes Your Brain: Breakthrough From a Leading Neurologist* (New York: Random Publishing House, 2009), 20.

4   James Fowler, *Stages of Faith: The Psychology of Human Development and the Quest for Meaning* (New York: Harper and Collins Publishers, 1981), 3.

5   Newberg and Waldman, 131–133.

6   Timothy Jennings, "The God Shaped Brain," *Rolling Hills Church*, June 15, 2013, video file, YouTube: https://www.youtube.com/watch?v=eA8ftVVyB-g.

7   Daniel Siegel. *Mindsight: The New Science of Personal Transformation* (New York: Bantam Books, the Random Publishing Group, 2010), 31–36.

8   Berne, Eric. "Games People Play, Part 1." *NET Science Broadcast Special*, video file, Feb. 6, 2011, YouTube: https://www.youtube.com/watch?v=NBO38HqQTgI.

9   Merle A. Fossum and Marilyn J. Mason, *Facing Shame: Families in Recovery* (New York: Norton and Company, 1986), 5.

10   Daniel Amen, "Kill the Ants," Amen Clinic, video file, Feb. 12, 2015, YouTube: https://www.youtube.com/watch?v=F90ljFspXu0.

11   Linda Graham, "Bouncing Back: Renewing the Brain," PESI INC, Feb. 12, 2009, YouTube: htps://www.youtube.com/watch?v=aPk6Eq-gssQ.

12   Lisa Firestone, "How Your Attachment Style Impacts Your Relationships," *Psychology Today*, July 30, 2013, https://www.psychologytoday.com/us/blog/compassion-matters/201307/how-your-attachment-style-impacts-your-relationship

Chapter 4: Attending: Being Present with or Aware of another

1   Timothy Jennings, "Healing the Mind, Session Five—the Brain Body Connection," Come and Reason Ministries, May 19, 2014.,Watch?=PLgl7roH977PFCe6rTCO-3xJDnP6Y&y_-3DOl9s41M.

2   Newburg and Waldman, 3.

3   Dean Ware, "Psychologist Guide to Emotional Well Being," *Dailyshoring*, Oct. 26, 2018, https://www.dailyshoring.com/neurons-that-fire-together-wire-together/

4   "Why Gratitude Can Be Good." *Greater Good Magazine*. https:// search ?q =greater+good+magazine&cvid=be520e862c484650b372c4381bf64 d3b &aqs=edge.1.69i59i45018.79958255j0j4& FORM=ANAB 01&PC=U531.

5   Robert A. Emmons and Michael E. McCullough, "Counting Blessings Versus Burdens: An Experimental Investigation of Gratitude and Subjective Well-Being in Daily Life," *Journal of Personality and Social Psychology*, 2003, vol. 84, no. 2, 377–389.

Chapter 5 Musings: A Time of Reflection or Thought

1   Phillip Keller, *A Shepherd Looks at Psalm 23* (Grand Rapids: Zondervan Publishing House, 1970), 60.
2   Keller, 69.
3   Keller, 74.
4   Pastor David, "Green Weekend: Transformation of South Africa" (Sermon, Reconciliation Networks of Our World, Coventry England, November, 1996)
5   Keller, 115.
6   Henry Blackaby, "Experiencing God," *Goodreads*, https://www.goodreads.com/work/quotes/41831464-experiencing-god-how-to-live-the-full-adventure-of-knowing-and-doing-the will of god/.
7   Arthur Golden, "Adversity," *Goodreads*, https://www.goodreads.com/quotes/18125-adversity-is-like-a-strong-wind-i-don-t-mean-just.
8   M. Scott Peck, *The Road Less Traveled: A New Psychology of Love, Traditional Values and Spiritual Growth* (New York: Simon and Schuster Inc., 1976), 83.
9   Mary Oliver, "Uses of Sorrow," *Poetry Friday*, Oct. 11, 2011. https://livelovesimple.com/the-uses-of-sorrow.
10 Henri J. M. Nouwen, *Love, Henri: Letters on the Spiritual Life* (New York: Crown Publishing, 2016), 72.
11 Siegel, *Mindsight*, 83.
12 Elesha Coffman, "What Luther Said," *Christianity Today International*, August 2008, https://www.christianitytoday.com/history/2008/august/what-luther-said.htm.
13 Qal Consecutive Imperfect: "was saying and continued to say." I've interpreted as a calling in the past with a continuing calling. That is, God spoke to Abram in Ur to Leave (1) his country, (2) his clan, and (3) his family. He was partially obedient—moving from his country and clan but not his family—along the Fertile Crescent, reaching Haran. He settled there until Terah died.

14 Qal perfect, completed action. God spoke only after they separated.

15 Charles   Haddon   Spurgeon,   "Trust   God,"
    Goodreads,   https://www.goodreads.com/
    quotes/1403154-god-is-too-good-to-be-unkind-and-he-is.

16 Exline Julie J. and Peter Hill. "Humility: A Consistent and Robust
    Predictor of Generosity." *The Journal of Positive Psychology* 7, no. 3
    (2011): 208-218.

17 William P. Young, *The Shack.* (Newberry Park: Windblown Media,
    2007), 97.

18 Siegel, *Mindsight,* xiii.

19 Siegel, *Mindsight,* xiii .

Chapter 6: Resurrection: The State of One Awakened from Death

1 G. Barna, "Research on How God Transforms Lives Reveal a Ten Step
   Journey," *Faith and Christianity*, March 27, 2011, https://www.barna.
   com/?s=+How+God+Transforms+Lives+Reveal+a+Ten+Step+Journey.

2 John Piper, *Filling Up the Afflictions of Christ: The Cost of Bringing the
   Gospel to the Nations in the Lives of William Tyndale, Adoniram Judson,
   and John Paton* (Wheaton, Illinois: Crossway Books, 2009), 22.

3 Parenthesis mine; verb is perfect passive indicative: crucified ongoing
   as if an actual fact.

4 Margery Williams Bianco, "The Velveteen Rabbit Quotes,"
   Goodreads, https://www.goodreads.com/work/quotes/1602074-the-
   velveteen-rabbit.

5 Fandom Entertainment. Interview. September 2, 2011. https://www.
   youtube.com/watch?v=G9QRz2D6nDA.

6 Everett Worthington, "An Evidence Based Group Intervention
   to Help Christian Couples Forgive" (Lecture, National American
   Association of Christian Counselors, September, 2015).

7   I've attempted to stay true to the meaning of the text while bringing it home to where we live. "Kingdom" as the thief purposed, reigning with Christ. "Paradise," Persian background, Eden, or You will be with Me just as God walked with Adam and Eve.

8   Jean Vanier, "Extraordinary Love," *Goodreads*, https://www.goodreads.com/quotes/38456-we-are-not-called-by-god-to-do-extraordinary-things.

9   Lit. "…have been already consummated." To me this helps to explain the request for vinegar.

10   "Bless the Broken Road" lyrics © Universal Music - Careers, Jeff Diggs Music

Appendixes

1   "List of Generic Negative and Positive Beliefs." *Emdtherapyvolusia*, https://emdrtherapyvolusia.com/wp-content/uploads/2016/12/Beliefs_Negative_Positive.pdf

2   Jason Marsh, "Tips for Keeping a Gratitude Journal," *Greater Good Magazine*, Nov. 17, 2011. https://greatergood.berkeley.edu/article/item/tips_for_keeping_a_gratitude_journal.

3   Newberg and Waldman, How God Changes Your Brain, 179–180.

4   Jennings, "The God Shaped Brain," 227.

5   Julie Axel, "Five Stages of Grief and Loss," *PscyhCentral*, https://psychcentral.com/lib/the-5-stages-of-loss-and-grief/.

6   Codependent Relationships: Symptoms, warning signs and behavior (medicalnewstoday.com).

Bibliography

Amen, Daniel. "Kill the Ants." *Amen Clinic.* Feb. 12, 2015. https://www.youtube.com/watch?v=F90ljFsPXu0.

Barna, G. "Research on How God Transforms Lives Reveal a Ten Step Journey." *Faith and Christianity.* March 27, 2011. https://www.barna.com/?s=+How+God+Transforms+Lives+Reveal+a+Ten+Step+Journey.

Baux, Millard. "Spirituality and Evangelism" (Sermon, Evangelism Conference, Fresno, CA, Jan. 20, 2001).

Berne, Eric. "Games People Play, Part 1." *NET Science Broadcast Special.* Feb. 6, 2011. https://www.youtube.com/watch?v=NBO38HqQTgI.

Bianco, Margery Williams. "The Velveteen Rabbit Quotes." *Goodreads.* https://www.goodreads.com/work/quotes/1602074-the-velveteen-rabbit.

Blackaby, Henry. "Experiencing God." *Goodreads.* https://www.goodreads.com/work/quotes/41831464-experiencing-god-how-to-live-the-full-adventure-of-knowing-and-doing-the will of god/.

Boyd, Laura. "How Do We Learn." *TED: Ideas worth spreading.* Nov. 15, 2015. https://www.youtube.com/watch?v=LNHBMFCzznE&t=4s.

Coffman. Elesha. "What Luther Said." *Christianity Today International.* August 2008. https://www.christianitytoday.com/history/2008/august/what-luther-said.htm.

David, Pastor (not real name). "Green Weekend: Transformation of South Africa." Sermon, Reconciliation Networks of Our World, Coventry England, November, 1996.

Eareckson Tada, Joni. DVD. February, 2011. Dr. Tim Clinton. American Association of Christian Counselors. Fairfax, Virginia: American Association of Christian Counselors.

Exline, Julie J., and Peter Hill. "Humility: A Consistent and Robust Predictor of Generosity." *The Journal of Positive Psychology* 7, no. 3, 2011.

Firestone, Lisa. "How Your Attachment Style Impacts Your Relationships." *Psychology Today.* July 30, 2013. https://www.psychologytoday.com/us/blog/compassion-matters/201307/how-your-attachment-style-impacts-your-relationship.

Fossum, Merle A., and Marilyn J. Mason. *Facing Shame: Families in Recovery.* New York: Norton and Company, 1986.

Fowler, James. *Stages of Faith: The Psychology of Human Development and the Quest for Meaning.* New York: Harper and Collins Publishers, 1981.

Golden, Arthur. "Adversity." *Goodreads.* https://www.goodreads.com/quotes/18125-adversity-is-like-a-strong-wind-i-don-t-mean-just.

Graham, Linda. "Bouncing Back: Renewing the Brain." *PESI INC.* February 12, 2009. htps://www.youtube.com/watch?v= aPk6Eq-gssQ.

Jennings, Timothy. "Healing the Mind, Session Five –the Brain Body Connection." *Come and Reason Ministries.* May 19, 2014. Watch?=PLgl7roH977PFCe6rTCO-3xJDnP6Y&y_-3DOl9s41M.

Jennings, Timothy. "The God Shaped Brain." Rolling Hills Church. Video File, June 15, 2013. https://www.youtube.com/ watch?v=eA8ftVVyB-g.

Keller, Phillip. *A Shepherd Looks at Psalm 23.* Grand Rapids: Zondervan Publishing House, 1970.

Marsh, Jason. "Tips for Keeping a Gratitude Journal." *Greater Good Magazine.* November 17, 2011. https://greatergood.berkeley.edu/ article/item/tips_for_keeping_a_gratitude_journal

Newberg, Andrew, and Mark Robert Waldman. *How God Changes Your Brain: Breakthrough Findings from a Leading Neuroscientist.* New York: Ballantine Books, 2009.

Nouwen, Henri J. M. *Love, Henri: Letters on the Spiritual Life.* New York: Crown Publishing, 2016.

Oliver, Mary. "Uses of Sorrow" *Poetry Friday.* Oct. 11, 2011. https:// livelovesimple.com/the-uses-of-sorrow.

Peck, M. Scott. *The Different Drum: Community Making and Peace.* New York: Simon and Schuster Publishers, 1987.

Peck, M. Scott. *The Road Less Traveled: A New Psychology of Love, Traditional Values and Spiritual Growth*. New York: Simon and Schuster Inc., 1976.

Piper, John. *Filling Up the Afflictions of Christ: The Cost of Bringing the Gospel to the Nations in the Lives of William Tyndale, Adoniram Judson, and John Paton*. Wheaton, Illinois: Crossway Books, 2009.

Sibcy, Gary. "Executive Function and Spiritual Growth." *Christian Counseling Today Magazine*.

Siegel. Daniel. *Mindsight: The New Science of Personal Transformation*. New York: Bantam Books, the Random Publishing Group, 2010.

Spurgeon, Charles Haddon. "Trust God." *Goodreads*.https://www.goodreads.com/quotes/1403154-god-is-too-good-to-be-unkind-and-he-is.

Vanier, Jean. *Community and Growth*, revised ed. New York: Paulist Press, 1989.

Wangerin Jr., W. *Ragman and Other Cries of Faith*. New York: Harper Collins, 1984.

Ware, Dean. "Psychologist's Guide to Emotional Well Being." *Dailyshoring*. October 26, 2018. https://www.dailyshoring.com/neurons-that-fire-together-wire-together/.

Young, William P. *The Shack*. Newberry Park: Windblown Media, 2007.

About the Author

Ethan James is a fictitious name used to insure the privacy of those in this book

The author has pastored in Flower Bluff, Texas; and in Oakland, Hayward, and Turlock, California.

He graduated with a Bachelor of Arts degree from the University of Corpus Christi, Texas; a Master of Divinity degree from Golden Gate Seminary, Mill Valley, California; and a Doctor of Ministry degree from Fuller Seminary, Pasadena, California.

He was chaplain to the Turlock Police Department. He also wrote a weekly advice column in a local newspaper, *The Manteca Bulletin*, and hosted a Sunday night call-in program on radio. He served as the on-site Intercession Prayer Facilitator and Co-Director for an international reconciliation program, Reconciliation Networks of Our World.

He has traveled extensively in the United States and globally, supporting local and international ministries, and facilitated numerous workshops on brain science and spirituality.

He opened Sonburst Counseling Services, As director, he extensively counseled clients affected by post-traumatic stress disorder due to sexual abuse, war, accidents, or complex grief. Through his training with a technique that stimulates the brain's hemispheres, allowing the mind to process trauma, he came to realize how much of our trust in God and relationships to others are impacted by our thinking.